Dedication

To all the people I'm blessed to call friend.

To my family. We didn't choose to be family, but you choose to inspire, motivate, guide, encourage, and love me – that means everything to me, thank you.

To my parents who continue to love and support me through all of life's surprises. Who raised me in faith to know the unwavering love of God. My mom who inspires me to be positive and seek the good in each situation and person.

To my son, Talon, his presence in my life has brought purpose and always encourages me to be the best version of myself.

To my best friend, the man I *get* to call husband, Steve. May we always laugh way more than we cry. It's six years post-amputation and this journey still feels new at times. I'm grateful for each day we're blessed with and look forward to continuing life with you. I choose you every day.

Contents

HIS BODY

OUR AMPUTATION

danette penrod

His Body Our Amputation
Published by The Elephant Sisterhood Publishing Company
Littleton, CO
Copyright @2022 Danette Penrod. All rights reserved.

Publisher's Cataloging-in-Production data
Names: Penrod, Danette, author
Title*: His Body Our Amputation* / by Danette Penrod
Description: First trade paperback original edition. {Littleton, Colorado}: The Elephant Sisterhood Publishing Company, 2022

Identifier: ISBN 979-8-9868907-0-8
Subjects: LCSH: Amputation, caretaking, family, spouse, caregiver, medical

Cover design by Danette Penrod, photography by Nikki Brooker Photography
Interior design with photography by Danette Penrod
Editor: Cynthia Young
Author Photo: Nikki Brooker Photography

Quantity Purchases: Long-term caretaker organizations and support groups, companies, professional groups, clubs, prosthetists, and other organizations may qualify for special terms when ordering quantities of this title.

For information email Hello@theelephantsisterhood.com.

The Prelude
(or Civic in this case)

"A woman is going to ask you a question that's going to change your life." I was working as a temp for Janus Mutual Funds and my cubemate, Lorraine, who was an intuitive, decided to drop that random thought on me. We chatted a little about it, I wanted to know what she was feeling and if she had thoughts around when it would happen. There wasn't a whole lot of information she could provide me, other than she thought it would be soon.

I was a 22-year-old living in Aurora, Colorado in my parents' basement. I had done the four-year college thing for a whopping semester and decided that particular college down in Texas wasn't for me. I moved home and finished out my freshman year at community college. I ended up graduating from the Colorado Institute of Art with a degree in video production, a love I had developed in high school. While at community college I started dating a man and after a year of dating he proposed. We were three-and-a-half years into dating when my life was about to change [according to my friend at Janus].

I was driving a Honda Civic SI that apparently was highly desirable, I walked out to go to work one morning and my car wasn't on the driveway. I looked around in disbelief and walked back inside to ask my dad if he moved it. I knew it was a dumb question, but I couldn't really make sense of what had happened. We both walked out to the driveway as if it were going to reappear, and sure enough, it was still gone. After calling my supervisor, Steve, to let him know I would be late and calling the police to file a report, my dad drove me to work.

I ended up being just a few minutes late. I sat down, got logged into the system, and almost immediately got a phone call. After concluding the conversation with the investor, Steve called me into his office. He had listened to my call, wanting to know if my head would be in the game given my morning events. We talked for a while about the call, my car, and some small talk. It was a nice reprieve from being on the phones, and I didn't mind his company either.

Fast forward a little over a month and my mom was driving me to pick up my car from the body shop. Yes, the police had found my car, it had been stripped of parts and had some body damage. We were almost to the dealership when my mom asked me "Why do you love Rob?" I sat there in silence, thinking in my head, *why do I love my fiancé?* After an awkward bit of silence, I simply responded, "I don't know."

I didn't realize it in that moment but that ended up being the question that changed my life. Rob and I had been dating for three and a half years but just six months earlier, after he canceled our second wedding date, he informed me that he was still legally married. She lived in Florida and we were in Colorado, so it wasn't a mistress-type situation, but still astounded that he didn't think that information was important to share - like on our first date!? Because we'd been together for three years before he told me, I tried to make it work. However, I was betrayed and couldn't get over it. I felt if he were going to lie to me for so long about something like that, what else would he lie to me about? I was so embarrassed and hurt that I couldn't bring myself to tell my parents or anyone else about this new truth. For me, the light was starting to dim on our relationship; meanwhile I was putting on a front for those around me, including him.

"Why can't I get this 'other' dude out of my head?" ... I thought to myself as I was trying to study for my Series 6 and Series 63 financial securities examinations. I was trying to solidify my job offer to work for Janus Mutual Funds as a fulltime employee, but every time I turned the page, it was like I was looking at a book of my life and I couldn't get this guy out of my head. The guy was Steve, my supervisor at Janus. I didn't know very much about him. I was attracted to his demeanor and just couldn't shake him from my mind. I had dreamed about us meeting, getting married, and even having a son – only problem was I was engaged to another man and didn't want kids, so it didn't seem remotely like a realistic thought.

While I was going through on-boarding at Janus, we were all shifted around to a new building for the training, so I wasn't around Steve, my temp supervisor anymore. I decided to open up a little to Lorraine, my "psychic" cubemate, about some of the things that were going on. She highly encouraged me to reach out to him, since I couldn't shake him from my thoughts. I wasn't sure what to say as I was still engaged, but I compiled an email seeing if he might want to meet me for a drink. I sat there reading the email over and over until Lorraine reached over and hit my hand down on the mouse which sent the email. Oh shoot! I was nervous with anticipation; would he even respond? About 15-minutes later I received an email back, "Sure we can rap."

We met at a Ruby Tuesday, ironically on a Tuesday, and had a great, but slightly awkward conversation. We addressed the typical stuff - talking about our childhoods, what brought us to Colorado, and things we enjoy. Then he asked me, "What's up with the ring?" Oops, I intentionally left it on, but was so caught up in the moment I'd forgotten about it. So, I was just honest about it. I told him about my three-and-a-half-year relationship, and the news I'd gotten six months prior. I shared how I'd checked out of the relationship a while ago but had been scared to let it go. There were lots of questions and I didn't hesitate to answer. I felt very comfortable.

After a few hours we decided to conclude our evening together. As I hugged him goodbye, I felt so comfortable and had a strong urge to kiss him but pulled away. He asked if we could connect again on Friday to which I replied, "I would love to, but..." And as I pointed at my engagement ring said, "Let me take care of something before I commit. I'll reach out tomorrow and we can go from there."

On my drive home I felt an overwhelming sense of joy. I knew what I needed to do. I walked through the garage door and my parents were sitting on the couch watching TV. My mom looked over and said Rob's called several times wondering where you were. I had told both he and my parents the truth, I was going to be studying after work and would be going out to dinner with a friend. I apologized to my parents that they had been bothered with the calls (this was pre cell phone by the way). My mom asked if I was okay, but the way she asked made me feel like she already knew the answer. I said I was great and receded to my basement bedroom. As I walked down the stairs, I removed my engagement ring and immediately picked up the phone. I called Rob and told him that I couldn't do this anymore.

I'm sure it felt completely out of the blue to him. I had outwardly put on a happy face over the past six months, but I was over it. He was distraught and wanted to come over and talk. I told him there was nothing to discuss. I'd made up my mind and explained how hurt I was to learn that he was still legally married, that he lied to me for three years and I just couldn't get over it. It was a short conversation. I was emotionally spent but felt a sense of peace – it was freeing.

The next day I had a pep in my step. I felt lighter and was so giddy to send Steve an email to let him know that I was free to hang out on Friday. It was a good day, no regrets about the breakup whatsoever. However, Rob was waiting for me when I got home from work. He wanted to talk things out, but there just wasn't anything to talk about. I gave him back the engagement ring, which was a huge trigger for him. I'm not sure if that made the breakup more of a reality for him or what, but his tone changed when I handed him the box. He started accusing me of cheating on him. I told him I'd been faithful and that I tried to get over the lies, but that I just couldn't do it anymore. He started yelling at me and continued to accuse me of being unfaithful. As I walked away and went back inside, I simply told him, "If that's what you need to tell yourself to help you get over me, so be it."

My parents were another story. They were so confused. Here I'd been dating a guy for three-and-a-half-years and without any sign of major struggle I broke off the engagement. I knew my parents would be angry at the situation and hurt for me, so I just told them that he lied to me and lost my trust and that although I tried, I just couldn't forgive him enough to marry him. To be honest, I think this was a relief to them. My parents were always supportive, but I knew they weren't huge fans of Rob and didn't think he was the right man for me.

I was glowing and happy, but I'd just broken up with the man I was going to marry, so my mom knew something was up. She asked me if I'd met another guy, to which I said "yes." She asked me if he was *the one* to which I also said "yes."

Steve and I officially started dating that Friday, September 1, 2000, and I literally never looked back. Things were so easy with him. We could sit in silence, we made each other laugh, we just got one another. Every relationship I had up to dating him was filled with bickering, stupid fights, and tears. The only tears I had with Steve were laughing so hard we cried and the overwhelming emotions I felt for him that morphed as tears of joy. It's amazing how easy things are when you're with the right person.

Fast-forward to April 1, 2002, we were married in a drive-thru in Las Vegas. It was totally planned though. We stayed at the Bellagio where we had our wedding photos done and had a reception in Colorado for our friends and family a week later. Over the next five years we enjoyed a pretty normal life – working, Steve played in multiple softball leagues, simple vacations, lots of house parties, and just enjoying our life together.

Remember how I dreamed that we met, got married and had a son? Well, on March 13, 2007, we welcomed our son, Talon, into the world. Although when we got married neither of us wanted kids, one day I came home from work and shared with Steve that my boss had asked me to become a Certified Financial Planner for him. It was a big deal and required more education and tests, so I jokingly said, "I just wanted to make sure you don't want to have a family, because this will be a huge commitment." To my complete surprise he quickly responded that he wanted to have a family. Oh dear, I thought, I literally had no desire to have a kid. It took me nearly a year of reflection, prayer, and tons of conversations to finally conclude that starting a family would be a wonderful blessing. And no, I didn't ever pursue the CFP designation.

As we fast forward through the next nine years it was a pretty standard life. We were a happy family, living our best life. Work, raising our son, family vacations, enjoying time with friends and family, Talon's school events and sports - nothing extraordinary, but loving every moment.

Family Dynamics

My parents, Steve's younger brother, Scott, and his family live in Colorado, about 20 minutes from the house we bought about two months after our marriage in 2002. Steve's family grew up in Illinois and despite our efforts to have his parents, Jon (father) and Carla (stepmom), join us in Colorado, they were content in the Midwest and didn't really seem to have a desire to move so we'd typically see them a couple times a year.

Like many, there's some family history and drama on Steve's side that you need a little insight into. (For the record I've got my own family drama, but I'll save those *Jerry Springer* tales for another book). The important thing to know is that Steve's dad and birth mom got divorced when he was four. The kids lived with their dad and saw their birth mom sporadically until Steve was about nine years old. Unfortunately, right around that time she stopped picking the kids up for a month straight and from that point on, Steve and his younger brother, Scott, decided not to go with her during her designated times. The boys were really too young to understand, but their older sister, Stacey, kept spending time with their mom, while they drifted further and further apart from her. [Since he hasn't had a relationship with his birth mom since he was nine, and his stepmom, Carla, came into the picture when he was six, when I talk about his mom going forward it will be his stepmom.] He also didn't have much to do with his sister, Stacey, since she moved out of the house to live with their birth mother when Steve was twelve. While there had been very little interaction with his sister while growing up, when Steve graduated high school and joined the Navy, ALL communication and interaction with his sister halted.

I have an older brother, so when Steve and I started dating and I learned he had a sister, I would ask about her. I didn't understand how he could have an older sister and not have anything to do with her. Despite my prying, all I ever got from Steve and his family was that she was selfish, always looking for a handout, and had emotionally hurt their dad very deeply.

For the most part I let it go, but every once in a while, I would question their lack of relationship. People change, she was young, Steve was even younger, the list in my head went on, but I treaded lightly when I would bring her up. Stacey attempted to connect with the brothers' wives through Facebook, but both Steve and Scott were adamant to not respond. When she turned forty, she wrote each of them a letter. I remember thinking it sounded like she was in AA (or something), going through *the steps* and trying to make amends. Those letters, like all other communication attempts, lead nowhere.

Also, it's important to note that in June of 2016, Steve's brother Scott had gotten into it with his mom about how they were raised, specifically, actions and treatment from her. The outcome was his mom crying and handing the phone over to his dad. Scott was told to have a nice f*ing life and hung up on. Shortly after, a letter came in the mail reaffirming that statement and essentially writing Scott and his family off. I had a good relationship with Steve's mom, Carla, and as a peacemaker, I attempted to help resolve the issue. Carla was very hurt to learn that she was perceived as less than an ideal mom. My efforts were unsuccessful and the communication between us began to get a bit spotty, as did the weekly conversations that Steve would have with his parents.

To catch you up at this point in our life, also in June of 2016 after having worked for the same financial advisor for fifteen years, they were merging with another firm and I was worried about my role within the new firm, so I switched jobs to work for a new firm in downtown Denver. After an abrupt change at Janus, Steve left the financial industry and had sifted through various craftsman jobs, working his way up to a superintendent for a couple of home builders, managed crews for a paint and drywall company, and was even self-employed for five years, doing primarily residential construction. After working for a company that took him out of state during the week for a year and a half, Steve settled into a facilities maintenance role at the Sports Authority corporate offices. Talon was nine, thriving in fourth grade at an elementary school just down the street from us and was big into lacrosse.

Disclaimer: *Throughout the rest of the book there are genuine text messages that have been used to convey the story. These indicated text message have not been altered from their original format and contain grammatical errors, misspellings, and/or wrong words.*

Out of the Blue

What a fun night! That was the thought that went through my head as I woke up on Saturday morning, September 3, 2016. We'd gone over to some friends' house for dinner. It was a great start to the long three-day, Labor Day, weekend. When Steve woke up, he called me into the bedroom to show me his extremely swollen ankles and legs. We were thinking maybe he'd had an allergic reaction or just consumed a lot of salt, but after discussing what he ate and drank for dinner, nothing stood out. He had enough swelling that he stepped on the scale and was 10lbs heavier! Wow, that's crazy we thought.

I happened to walk into the bathroom just as he finished his morning "Austin Powers pee" and noticed that the toilet was nearly overflowing with bubbles. I asked him what the frothy urine was all about and how long it had been going on. He said maybe a couple weeks. I told him I thought it was protein in his urine and that he needed to make an appointment at the doc ASAP. He doubted me, asking why or how on earth I'd come to that conclusion. The only thing I can say is late in my pregnancy with Talon when I started to show edema, I was tested for protein in my urine. I wasn't sure, of course, I thought it sounded good and just knew that something wasn't right.

The following morning, Sunday, September 4, Steve woke up and his swelling didn't look any better. As a matter of fact, he was quite the sight - he was now bloated in his midsection too. So, he decided to step on the scale again and he'd gained another 10lbs! Although this was genuinely concerning Steve wasn't about to go to urgent care or the emergency room, which were the only options with it being a holiday weekend.

We were both worried what Monday morning would bring, but thankfully his weight gain slowed down and he was "only" 2lbs heavier. However, that was 22lbs in three days. Steve had a plan to call the doctor first thing Tuesday morning, so we chilled and enjoyed our vacation day with the fam and tried not to worry about Steve's condition.

Thankfully, Steve was able to get in with our primary care doctor on Tuesday, September 6. They did blood work, a urinalysis, and gave him an EKG. They thought that the upper valves in his heart were working harder than the lower, so he was instructed to make an appointment with a cardiologist. He did and that appointment was scheduled for November 3. Wait, what!?! It's only the first part of September, you could have a heart issue, but you can't get in to see a doctor for two months?

On Thursday, September 8, around 6:45 pm - we remember fairly vividly because it was the first Denver Broncos game of the regular season and we were with our neighbors watching the game. The PCP called and said that he wasn't sure about his lab results. With the initial results he was concerned about his liver and instructed him to stop drinking alcohol immediately. I literally watched this puppy dog pout come over his face as he poured his beer down the kitchen sink. Oh, and no ibuprofen. The doc also wanted him to come back and have more blood work done to rule out hepatitis. When he told us that his urinalysis didn't show protein, I questioned the results and said I was shocked. We chatted about what I'd seen with the froth in the toilet and that seemed to get his attention. He asked Steve how far away we were from the office and asked if he could meet him at the clinic in 15 minutes. Steve met up with the PCP around 7 pm and he ended up doing two more urinalysis - both yielded VERY high levels of protein, which meant Steve needed to make an appointment with a nephrologist, a kidney specialist, as soon as possible. He also went ahead and prescribed him 20mg of Lasix, to help with the edema, and was told to get it filled and start taking it that night.

Unfortunately, the 20mg didn't do anything, so the next night he was instructed to take 40mg, rest and elevate his legs as much as possible over the weekend.

Minimal Change Disease

There is an exclusive, invitation-only golf course, The Sanctuary, in Castle Pines, Colorado. Because of Steve's love for golf and never having been extended an invitation to play until now, he decided to play despite the extra 22lbs of water weight he was now carrying. He had a wonderful time, but as you can imagine any amount of walking with the added water weight tired him out. After chillin' on the couch for about 30 minutes, he developed the awful charley horse in his right thigh. I had Steve get on the ground so I could really get into position to massage the spasms. When I applied pressure to the cramp Steve literally screamed at me that it moved and pointed to the new location. When I started to massage the new location, Steve screamed that it had moved, again. Confused, I jumped down to his feet and started massaging his entire leg by pulling down from his thigh to his toes. It took several minutes, but the pain subsided and the charley horse was gone.

On Monday, September 12, Steve was able to get in with the kidney specialist (nephrologist) for the first time. He, of course, had blood work and another urinalysis which again showed very high levels of protein. The doctor quickly assessed that Steve was an otherwise healthy 44-year-old. With the symptoms coming on so quickly he knew we needed to work fast to figure out the root cause. Through a panel of bloodwork, it was revealed that his kidneys while filtering out toxins were also leaking protein. The nephrologist ordered more blood work, an ultrasound of his legs and abdomen to rule out blood clots, as well as a kidney biopsy.

He also agreed with the Lasix prescription the PCP had prescribed but lowered the dose back down to 20mg and added potassium. Steve was also put on a 50oz per day fluid restriction and could only eat 2g of salt. The goal was to help him lose the water weight quickly, but as healthy as possible.

Thankfully, Steve was able to get in for a kidney biopsy the next day (Tuesday, September 13). All went well with the procedure, just a little nausea and killer headache from the anesthesia. It took a couple of days to get the results from the biopsy and, unfortunately, the results came back when the nephrologist was out of the country. So, the call didn't happen until September 19, which was the same day Steve had an ultrasound done from his neck down to again check his lungs, heart and assess for blood clots. The ultrasound images revealed nothing of concern, but the biopsy showed that Steve had Minimal Change Disease.

Minimal Change Disease (MCD), in non-clinical language, is a rare kidney disease, typically in children, that causes the kidneys to spill protein into urine. Protein is the body's natural anticoagulant, so blood clotting can become an issue. And since MCD is typically in kids the doctor said that more than likely there's a larger health issue going on with MCD being secondary. More blood work was ordered to rule out AIDS and Steve had a chest x-ray to rule out lung cancer. Both came back negative, but this meant there were no answers and the doctor was puzzled.

More on MCD: According to UNC School of Medicine [unckidneycenter.org], Minimal Change Disease (MCD for short) is a kidney disease in which large amounts of protein is lost in the urine. It is one of the most common causes of the Nephrotic Syndrome worldwide. The kidneys normally work to clean the blood of the natural waste products that build up over time. To do this they have to filter all of the blood in the body many times each day. That is in fact what urine is- filtered blood. Normally, the kidneys can filter this blood without losing any of the proteins that are supposed to remain in circulation. When the kidney filters are damaged, however, protein sometimes "slips through" into the urine. This is called proteinuria.

First ER Visit

On Saturday, September 24, Steve complained about his right calf hurting. He said it was super tight and felt like it could seize at any moment. By Sunday that feeling had extended from his calf to include his shin and top of his foot. Talon had a lacrosse game that morning and I remember Steve standing and trying to stretch it for over an hour while we watched the warm-ups and game. When he sat in our SUV going home, the pain was so sharp that he was nearly screaming, and there was no way he could drive.

After an agonizing 30-minute drive home, the weather had warmed up so he changed into shorts and flip flops. That's when I could see that his toes and top of his foot were purple. I leaned over to get a closer look and touch it – the top of his foot was ice cold. I told him I thought it could be a blood clot and that we should probably go to the ER. In typical male fashion (sorry hon) he said no and decided to call his PCP who also suggested the ER to get an ultrasound, so off we went.

The emergency room visit was short and uneventful. They ordered an x-ray of his right foot to rule out a stress fracture, an ultrasound was done starting from his groin and going down his right leg to look for any clots, and they did some basic blood work. No fracture, no clot, but he was a little low in calcium so they administered a calcium drip and said he could go home. They were literally pushing us out of the door with no answers when I finally thought to ask for pain meds. I mean despite them not finding anything, my man was still in excruciating pain. They basically shrugged off my request because Steve had refused pain medications from them earlier but ended up giving him six Vicodin. The only other instructions were to return to the ER if his symptoms didn't clear or got worse within a week.

Here is the update sent to family via text:
Date: Sunday, September 25, 2016 at 3:21 PM
Sorry for the delay, I don't get reception in the room. They just took Steve up to have an ultrasound done to check for blood clots. The X-ray on his foot came back fine. And they also just took some (more) blood work, to check electrolytes & potassium levels. I'll let you know when I hear more. He's still in a lot of pain, but refused the pain medication...

The second we got into our SUV to go home, Steve popped a Vicodin and leaned the seat back in an attempt to find a comfortable position. Unfortunately, the meds did nothing for the pain, and he was in so much of it that he opted to attempt to sleep on the couch that night to prevent disturbing me. At some point that night, he lost 6lbs and his right leg was back to normal size. The next day he had a regularly scheduled follow-up appointment with the nephrologist. I was working downtown, so I met him at the doctor's office, only I beat him there and I was running a little behind. Worried I called him, thankfully he was onsite, but it was taking him a while to get to the office because he kept having to stop because the pain in his right leg was just awful and it was shooting pain into his hip.

The doctor was extremely nonchalant about it, saying if it was a blood clot that his foot would be cold and his toes would be turning colors. That's when I responded with, "Yes, that's exactly why we took him to the ER!" He then said if it was blood clots that Steve wouldn't be sitting there because the pain would be so bad and that we had to trust the ultrasound that he'd ordered earlier on as well as the ER images. He concluded that the pain was due to muscle cramps from dehydration. He lifted his food and fluid restrictions and told him to stop taking the Lasix. He was also told to drink plenty of fluid that night and have a lot of salt. Steve ended up drinking 80oz of Gatorade and several glasses of water from about 3:30 pm until bedtime, he also did a shot of pickle juice as well as ate a salty Chinese dinner.

Here is the update sent to family via text:
Date: Monday, September 26, 2016 at 3:34 PM
Steve had his follow-up with the kidney specialist this afternoon. His blood work & chest x-ray were all negative (good). After his trip to the ER yesterday (which they did nothing & sent him home in pain) his Dr is certain that it's dehydration - he's still in intense pain today. He's having him stop his diuretic as well as food & water restrictions. He has a CAT scan tomorrow for one last rule out (Hodgkins Lymphoma) for the doc to feel confident that his minimal change disease is the only thing going on. Thank you for your continued prayers & support. We love you all & are so grateful for our support system.

The following day, Tuesday, September 27, the pain was so bad that unannounced Steve decided to go back to the nephrologist to let him know that his efforts, with all the fluid intake, had not worked and how much worse he'd gotten.

The nephrologist once again dismissed him and told him that he was suffering from severe dehydration in his calf muscle and that the muscle was shrinking and pulling on the tendons in his foot, which was causing the blood flow to be interrupted.

Steve suffered all day with no changes. I suggested seeing an acupuncturist to try to loosen the muscle. He reluctantly made an appointment and tried acupuncture two days in a row. Apparently neither appointment was pleasant or successful, so Steve decided to go back to his primary care doctor. The PCP prescribed 350mg of Carisoprodol, which is a muscle relaxer and suggested that he should get an MRI and that someone would call him to get it set up.

Unfortunately, no one ever called, so Steve called back the next day, now Friday, September 30. He had to leave a message and once again no one called to follow-up to get the MRI scheduled. The weekend was much of the same - TONS of pain and no relief. This also meant no sleep, so Steve was beyond mental and physical exhaustion at this point. Still camped out on the couch in the basement in attempts to find relief and sleep any chance he could.

On Monday, October 3, Steve called his PCP back again about getting the MRI scheduled. The PCP was overly concerned about how much pain he was still in and suggested that he go back to the ER to have an MRI where they could get and read the results immediately. Steve called me at work, I left early and I opted to take him to a different hospital this time around.

Here is the update sent to family via text:
Date: Monday, October 3, 2016 at 9:31 AM
Leaving work and taking Steve to ER at Anschutz. No idea what's going to happen. May need help with Talon, but I'll let you know.

No Pulse

Within 45 minutes of arriving at the new hospital's emergency department, they had six vascular team members in the room because no one could find a pulse in his right foot. They ordered an ultrasound and CT scan, and it was only a few minutes of waiting before the ultrasound tech got there. Although the technician couldn't read the results to us, he said he thought we'd hear the words "surgery" before the day was up. Immediately following the ultrasound, they took Steve out to have the CT scan. Within 20 minutes of his CT scan a plain-clothed surgeon came in to discuss his unique case.

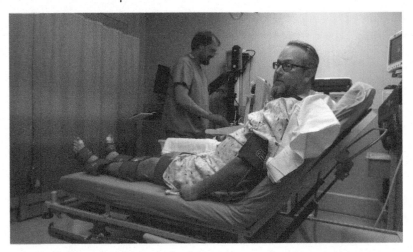

Steve DID have a blood clot. In fact, he had a few. They found a dangling clot in the aorta coming out of his stomach, a blood clot in his right thigh, and a blood clot in the back of his knee that also appeared to be in the tops of the three arteries leading down his right leg. Needless to say, he was admitted to the hospital for pain management and vascular surgery.

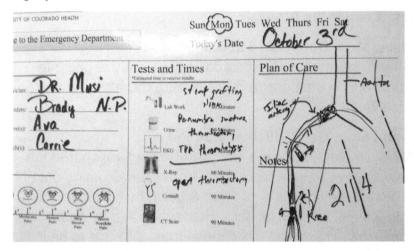

I had been texting with Steve's family and my parents with the details of what was going on. I called our neighbor, Mr. Jerry, to see if he could pick Talon up from school and see if he'd be willing to spend the night at our house and get him off to school the next morning. He was more than happy to help, which was so reassuring. My brain was mush, I remember the emergency room details vividly that day, but I honestly have no recollection of the stay in the hospital that night or what I said to our son.

Here are the updates sent to family via text:
Date: Monday, October 3, 2016 at 12:01 PM
We're in the ER & he's on a 2nd doc... waiting now for the vascular team to come see him, since they can't find a pulse in his right foot.

Date: Monday, October 3, 2016 at 3:02 PM
Jerry is going to take care of Talon this afternoon/evening.
I'm not sure how long we'll be here, but they are going to
admit him to the hospital...

Date: Mon, Oct 3, 2016 at 3:06 PM
Steve's getting his CT scan done now. They're going to
admit him to the hospital & make sure this issue gets
resolved.

Date: Mon, Oct 3, 2016 at 4:36 PM
CT scan came back & a 4th vascular surgeon shared the
news. Steve has 3+ blockages: in the aorta coming out of his
stomach, behind his right knee & down by his ankle going
into 3 small veins in his foot. He's scheduled for surgery
tomorrow. There's a 75% chance that he'll have to be in ICU
for 48 hours due to the medicine they'll likely have to give
him to take care of the small vein blockages. There's a whole
lot more to this, but this is it in a nutshell. Steve is beside
himself as you can imagine, but we're extremely grateful it
was caught this way vs a stroke. Thank you for all the
prayers. I'll be in touch more soon.

Date: Tuesday, October 4, 2016 at 7:19 AM
He didn't sleep well, as you can imagine, but he's
"comfortable" & relaxed.

Date: Tuesday, October 4, 2016 at 7:39 AM
Thanks! Yes, we talked this morning about things. The
vascular team just came in - we still don't have a time yet &
might not know until an hour before. Sigh!

Date: Tuesday, October 4, 2016 at 2:15 PM
Steve is in pre-op now...

On Tuesday, October 4, around 2:15 pm. Steve headed into his first surgery. There was a lot to be done - they put a stent graft over the dangling clot in the artery coming out of his stomach, a catheter from his left groin over to and down to his right leg and used TPA (Tissue Plasma Activator) medicine to try to clear out the clot in his thigh and behind his right knee.

Nearly six hours later, the surgeon emerged from the operating room to share the news. They were successful with the stent graph and were able to clear out about 70% of the clot in his thigh. However, the clot behind his knee didn't budge. He was admitted to the Intensive Care Unit (ICU) since he had to lay flat on his back and not move as they left the catheter in place and continued to drip the TPA medicine into his right leg. ICU was also necessary because the TPA medicine has to be monitored at all times – it can cause strokes, brain damage or cerebral bleeding. However, it's also a clot busting medicine, so the ICU stay seemed worth the risks.

Update texted to family post-surgery:
Date: Tuesday, October 4, 2016 at 7:43 PM
Dr just came out. There was success with 2 of the clots, but the 3 clots in the small veins behind his knee didn't budge. So he'll be in ICU for a couple days while they monitor the medicine that he needs to dissipate those clots. He'll have a procedure done tomorrow afternoon (like pictures) that will tell them how the medicine is working.

Intensive Care Unit

The first night in ICU was uncomfortable with next to no sleep – machines beeping and buzzing, every hour check-ins, and Steve's discomfort kept him in and out of consciousness. Meanwhile I'm freezing, trying to sleep curled up in a chair with an ottoman and my brain is running wild with the most horrific thoughts. I try to be a positive person, but my imagination and fear got the better of me more than once as I planned out my husband's funeral in my head.

Here are the updates sent to family via text to recount the first day in ICU leading up to the second surgery:
Date: Wednesday, October 5, 2016 at 7:12 AM
Steve nor I got much sleep last night. His nurse came in every hour for tests (she was quiet & left the lights off), but every time Steve stopped breathing for a moment his machines started buzzing - that happened a lot earlier on in the night due to the medication. Then it was just a matter of noise, discomfort, etc. His docs just came in for their morning rounds. They were able to find a faint pulse in 1 of 2 veins (the 3rd is too deep inside the foot to listen to) which is a good sign that the meds are working on those clots. This afternoon (no time, he's the 2nd case again today) they have to knock him out again so he'll go back to the operating room so they can look inside to see what's really happening.

Date: Wednesday, October 5, 2016 at 8:03 AM
Okay, Steve's surgeon just came in. The clotting he was able to suction out yesterday was a couple weeks old (consistency of a pencil eraser). Unfortunately, the meds, although worth a try, don't typically work on old clots. So, Steve will be going back to surgery, they will see what the meds have done to loosen it up but will more than likely have to do angioplasty (ballooning) to try to open those veins up in order to get flow. The Dr has a 7-8 hour surgery ahead of him today & Steve's will take 4-5 hours. So, it will likely be after 10pm before I have another report unless something else changes.

Breathing in-and-out...and staying positive. Steve's mindset is to "get'er done"

So grateful for all your support, love & prayers.

Date: Wednesday, October 5, 2016 at 6:27 PM
Just waiting for them to come get Steve for his surgery...

Date: Wednesday, October 5, 2016 at 7:19 PM
They finally started the pre-op stuff. Still sounding like it could be a 4-5 hour surgery once it actually starts.

Date: Wednesday, October 5, 2016 at 8:19 PM
They're just now taking him into the operating room...

It was about five hours later, now nearly 1 am (October 6), I could hear Steve in a rowdy voice, cussing at someone in the hallway. When they wheeled him back into the ICU room, he was alert and angry, so angry. From what I could gather he was convinced the anesthesiologist was a total jerk, but I couldn't really make heads or tails of what he was accusing him of. As several nurses worked to get him reconnected to all the machines, he looked over at me and said no one cares about him. He asked where he was and what he was doing there. I walked up to his bedside and placed my hand on his shoulder to try to comfort him and start explaining, but before I could get anything out of my mouth he started yelling "No one cares about me!" I was totally taken aback and confused with what was going on, so I just went back over to my chair and sat and watched as the nurses did their thing.

About that time the surgeon came in to chat with me about the results of the second surgery. He was successful in getting the clot in the thigh to dissipate, but the clotting behind the knee was stubborn and basically from his knee down to his toes was one gigantic clot. He told me that we needed the TPA medicine to work, but that it doesn't work well on old clotting. So, I asked him, "What is considered old clots?" In the blood world "old" is just a couple days. I remember specifically asking him if Steve had these blood clots a week ago when I took him to the emergency department. He never did answer me directly with a definitive yes, but repeated that based on the consistency and severity of the clotting it would appear that the clots were one to three weeks old. My head was spinning, as I started replaying our first ED visit in my head. "Doc, if they are old clots and the medicine doesn't work, what does that mean?" I finally asked. His words were crystal clear. He was confident that Steve would not be looking at an amputation situation now or ever. Whew!

The conversation wasn't long, and I was quickly thrust back into the drama at hand. After about an hour-long rant of cussing, yelling, and making statements about no one caring about him, Steve finally seemed to calm down, when all of a sudden, his machines started going crazy.

Four ICU nurses ran into the room to see what was going on. I was already bedside and could see that he was choking. One of the nurses tried to get the vacuum to suck out whatever it was that was obstructing his airway, but the machine wouldn't turn on. She started to mess with the power cord, while I ran to the sink, grabbed some paper towels and ran back over and scooped out his mouth. Coughing commenced and all I saw was blood and his machines had fallen silent.

"What's going on? What's happening?" were the thoughts racing in my head. My husband is going to die from choking on his own blood in front of me. That's when I got a bit elevated and started yelling "Why is there blood? Why is he choking on blood?" A nurse got me back in my chair and quickly and calmly the four nurses finished clearing out his mouth, got him reconnected and there was a moment of calm. I sat on the edge of my chair scared and staring in disbelief.

All of the nurses left and the next several hours was like a broken record of Steve asking or yelling the same question over and over again at me and/or anyone in the room. His memory was about 30-seconds long, so he'd ask, we'd tell him, he'd forget and get angry again because in his brain nobody cared about him and no one was offering him answers, including me. I felt hopeless as thoughts of the movie *50 First Dates* played through my mind – was this going to be my life? Although my version was bleaker than the rom-com made a memory issue seem.

At some point during all this it was explained to me that there were complications during the surgery with anesthesia. They attempted to give him twilight anesthesia - which is an anesthetic technique where a mild dose of general anesthesia is applied to induce anxiolysis (anxiety relief), hypnosis, and anterograde amnesia (inability to form new memories). The patient is not unconscious but sedated. However, Steve was moving around too much and trying to talk, so they hurriedly stuck a tube down his throat to knock him out completely. In the emergent switch to get him unconscious, the tube sliced into his tongue.

Since I had no idea what twilight anesthesia was, I still didn't understand the memory issues and anger, but this shed some light on where the blood had come from, though the timing seemed strange. The only thing I could surmise was that at some point he aggravated the cut on his tongue enough that it started bleeding enough to choke. It was such a hard night, and he ended up having three panic attacks too.

Here are the updates sent to family via text about the second surgery:
Date: Thursday, October 6, 2016 at 12:42 AM
Surgery is done. Honestly not sure what to say. They didn't get the response they were hoping for - the blockages are all down his leg & throughout his foot in microscopic areas they can't surgically get to. He was able to get more of the clot out of the thigh, so the medication has been focused behind the knee & he said "we need the meds to work, we don't have another option."

On a positive note: Steve's body is somehow figuring out a way to get some blood flow through his foot, so the doc said that this is not now or should ever be a loss of limb situation. If the meds don't work then he'll have potentially lifelong debilitating pain.

Next step will be to do "pictures" tomorrow, maybe around 4 to check the progress of the meds.

Date: Thursday, October 6, 2016 at 7:35 AM
The docs just came by to do their rounds. They were able to find a decent pulse in a place that hasn't had one since he got here...that means something is working. Be it meds or Steve's body making its own path.

The plan is the same - he'll go back in later today for them to figure out how well things are flowing. More than likely, he said they would remove the catheter that's inside his leg (administering the meds) because if they haven't worked at the level, they were hoping it's not worth keeping him on it because the risks are too high. I believe this med is the only reason he's in ICU.

The best way I can describe what's going on is that a tree has a trunk, branches, twigs & leaves. The doc can operate on the trunk & branches, but it's Steve's "twigs & leaves" that are the issue.

Steve's starting to show mental fatigue & am doing what I can to keep him encouraged. Pray not just for better blood flow results, but also for his mental stability. I'm struggling to process what he's having to endure here & am so proud of him for his strength.

Date: Thursday, October 6, 2016 at 8:24 AM
Not entirely sure yet. From what the doc told me last night it could be extremely painful for the foreseeable future (possibly life), especially if he tried to jog or run...that part is not a problem.

Date: Thursday, October 6, 2016 at 8:37 AM
Last night was soooo hard. Steve had 3 panic attacks. Not to mention a barrage of other things that were so difficult to see/hear.

The harshness of the anesthesia gradually wore off, but Steve continued to have a hard day. His memory was all over the board with rather lucid moments and then fogginess. He was in a ton of pain, but the doctors were hopeful that meant blood flow was returning to his lower leg and foot. Around 2:30 in the afternoon Steve's blood pressure got so low that he had to have a blood transfusion. While that was scary, my mind was affixed to the thought that at some point, today, they would be taking him into his third surgery and I couldn't even imagine what to expect with the anesthesia. We had some positive news as they were able to find pulses in his foot and it felt physically warmer to the touch.

Tiger in ICU

Around 5:30 in the evening they told me it would still be a couple more hours before they could get him back on the operating table. While they couldn't give me a timeframe on how long the third surgery would be, their plan was to take the TPA catheter out and close him up, which meant the end was in sight for leaving ICU. I asked to speak to the anesthesiologist and let her know what a horrific experience he'd had with the twilight and going completely under combo. She assured me that she had a better plan. While Steve was in surgery the newest ICU nurse came on shift and was so sweet to come check on me. With the drama from the previous night, I prepped her and pre-apologized if he yelled at her or wasn't himself. I told her how sweet and funny he is and that last night's debacle wasn't the norm.

About two hours after they'd taken Steve in for his third surgery they wheeled him back in the room, I was shocked, and honestly infuriated, that he was completely naked with a part of a sheet barely covering his junk. The nurse must have seen the look on my face as she explained that it was all she could do to keep him covered. He was complaining about being hot, but I noticed his demeanor was very calm. He was talking about baseball and wanted an update on that evening's playoff game. "Okay," I thought to myself, this is definitely better than last night's anger.

A side note: the Chicago Cubs were in the playoffs fighting to make it to the World Series. Steve is a Cubs fan, from

Illinois originally, and has never wavered from them despite the disappointments year after year.

The new ICU nurse, the one I warned about anger issues, entered the room and immediately began to get him covered up and the lovely hospital gown put back on. Steve was totally hitting on her (can't blame him, she was very attractive). I don't recall exactly the nonsense he was saying until...

He looked her in the eyes, put up his hand and swatted at her ever so gently as if he had paws while saying "I'm a tiger...grrrrrr!" Oh, my goodness! The nurse and I both started cracking up.

At some point the surgeon came in to share that there was a huge improvement from the night before. He explained that the previous night he used the TPA medicine like a pressure washer and really went to town on one of his arteries in his leg. It worked, because the clotting in Steve's thigh was gone, one of the arteries in his legs was cleared down to about his ankle and the other two arteries had some improvement. They decided to give Steve's body a rest and leave the TPA drip in place to let it (hopefully) clear out more of the clotting.

The night was very smooth, Steve was able to go to sleep and all things considered, slept seemingly well.

More details about the day and results of the third surgery via my text messages:
Date: Thursday, October 6, 2016 at 10:06 PM
They JUST took Steve down for surgery...

Date: Thursday, October 6, 2016 at 11:58 PM
Well they're already done for tonight. They only took pictures...they noticed a HUGE improvement from last night's surgery. One of the veins had cleared down to his ankle, his thigh was 100% clear & the other 2 veins showed improvements too. So instead of "working" on him tonight they're going to allow the medicine to do its thing for the remaining time (remember it can only be used for 72hrs max). He'll have to remain in ICU, but this is great news. Prayers are being answered!

Getting Out of ICU

Around 6:30 am (October 7) the nurse asked him if he wanted something to eat. This was the first time he was allowed to eat or drink in 5 days, but he only had until 8 am! Steve wasn't shy when he ordered, he enjoyed bacon, eggs, toast, fruit, tapioca pudding and two glasses of orange juice. They wanted the TPA medicine to be administered as long as possible, so the day was long and uneventful. They came to get him for his final surgery about 9:30 pm.

The fourth surgery took over six hours, so Steve didn't return to the ICU room until after 3:30 am. During this time, I tried to catch up on sleep. The one benefit to Steve having the late-night surgeries was that, if my nerves allowed, it's when I should have been asleep in normal life. I often found myself drifting asleep in the middle of my prayers.

The time spent in ICU was the loneliest I've ever felt in my life. My family and friends were supportive, don't get me wrong, but in that room during the late-night surgeries when my family and friends were home asleep, I felt physically cold and mentally alone. It also felt as if time was standing still. It had been the longest five days of my life.

The update from the surgeon was a mixed bag. The extended time with the TPA drip did not yield any results, however, he worked extremely hard to ensure Steve the most success. He was able to open up all the veins leading into his foot, including being able to hear and feel a good pulse. There were a lot of blockages from the ankle down to his toes and there was no more progress with any of the arteries, plus there was no guarantee that the clotting wouldn't build back up. He also warned me that Steve would be in a lot of pain, so once released from ICU he would be admitted to the hospital to help with pain management and more than likely some physical therapy.

Update about the fourth surgery to the family via text:
Date: Saturday, October 8, 2016 at 3:39 AM
4th surgery is over. The last 24hrs of clot busting meds yielded no additional help. However, the Dr worked extremely hard in tonight's surgery to ensure Steve the most success. He was able to open up all veins leading into his foot, including being able to hear/feel a good pulse. There's still a lot of blockage from ankle down to his toes & he'll have a rough road ahead.

Over the next several days he'll have to learn how to pain manage, probably do some PT, & heal. They cannot guarantee that the blockages they were able to open up tonight are going to stay open. Steve's body is going to have to heal itself at this point.

The goal is for him to rest over the next few hours & try to get him out of ICU.

Because the surgery went into the wee hours of the morning, the morning rounds around 7 am came quick. They were happy with Steve's pulses. He had to do some strength tests, which were painful, but they said that the strength in his toes was good news. They said the goal was to get Steve sitting up and moved out of ICU to what they considered an intermediate floor, meaning he still needed to be monitored regularly and would have to do continued lab work to monitor his blood levels.

That's exactly what they did. The nurses came in and disconnected Steve from as many of the machines as they could and checked for bed sores. When they did, I noticed what looked like massive bruising on each of his upper thighs and across his lower abdomen. And then I saw "it" too! There was so much blood pooling from all the surgeries that his testicles were enlarged. I don't just mean moderately; I mean all the nurses were called in to have a look and a couple wanted to take a picture. Steve obviously couldn't see what all the fuss was about, so I told him he had an eggplant between his legs. We all laughed and it felt good to have a little humor brought into the room.

Not long after getting Steve sat up, he was able to order and enjoy breakfast. Funny how the little, but normal things in a hospital setting can feel so good. A couple hours after the morning rounds a new vascular surgeon was introduced to Steve and brought up to date with his journey. This allowed us to ask some questions too. We learned that he would probably be in the hospital until Tuesday or Wednesday, but even after his release he would probably be ten plus days out of being able to return to work. It sounded like they were planning on Steve having physical therapy, possibly at home, and that it was going to be a longer road than we'd expected to a full recovery.

Late afternoon Steve's aunt and uncle came to visit. We always laugh when we're with them and this visit was no different. The continued shift in energy was welcomed – and it was undeniable to me. The room felt physically warmer and brighter. Steve couldn't wait to offer to show off his ginormous eggplant to his uncle. After some bantering, and there may have even been a wager, he took a peek and confirmed the large vegetable. Tee-hee! We shared the proposed thoughts and plans for the coming weeks and his aunt and uncle were still with us when Steve was finally moved out of ICU just before 5 pm on Saturday (10/8). His pain was under control and his spirits were high, which allowed me to feel comfortable enough, for the first time in 6 days to go home and see Talon. Plus, his brother had graciously offered to come stay with Steve.

It was emotional for me as I pulled up to pick up Talon. He'd been spending the nights with a buddy from school. I hadn't spoken to him much, but the few times I did I knew he was confused, scared and uncomfortable. At first, as in the first night, it was fun to spend the night with a friend. Until the realization set in that they still had to go to school, his dad was in the hospital, his mom not around, and he was expected to resume life as a normal fourth grader while being completely out of his routine. It was challenging to say the least. I remember he said he missed his bed, our house, my cooking, and didn't like not getting to see or hug us every day.

Update to the family via text:
Date: Sunday, October 9, 2016 at 8:03 AM
Just talked to Steve (Scott spent the night). Sounds like things are all about the same. He got a little more sleep last night, & doing well with keeping pain under control.

This is when he's mentally going to start having a hard time with being in the hospital. So please pray for his patience & understanding.

Moving on Up, Er...Down

Steve was doing well enough that on Sunday (October 9) just after 6:30 pm they decided to move his room again, this time down to the lower floor, which means a patient is on their way to being discharged. He wasn't hooked to a bunch of machines and they only came in to do vitals every 4 hours, which allowed Steve to sleep for longer periods of time. Which he needed. He was so exhausted and unmotivated over the next couple days; it was hard to watch. The edema he had from all the surgeries and laying flat wasn't helping either.

Now that Steve wasn't umbilical corded to machines and with the imminent danger from the ICU behind us, we decided it was time to allow Talon to come visit. It was a mix of emotions. Steve wanted to see his son, but not while in a hospital bed. The innocence of Talon not understanding what his dad had just gone through and Steve wanting to put on a happy face and mask the reality of the unknown. My parents brought Talon in the room and Steve's emotional release was gut wrenching for all of us to watch.

About 24 hours after being removed from all the machines Steve's pain returned with a vengeance. From Monday (October 10) into Tuesday Steve didn't sleep. I was glad to have been with him, as he seemed to need something constantly - water, ice, phone charger, blanket, you name it. His pain was unbearable and his anxiety sent him into several tail spins more than once. Not to mention the surgeon showed up at 6:40 am on Tuesday (October 11) to give us a plan of action. He wanted a kidney specialist and hematologist to talk to us and was hopeful he would be discharged. He shed some light on the pain, stating it was due to the clots that remain in foot, which means lack of blood flow. He said it would take weeks for Steve's body to build collateral channels for proper blood flow.

The day of discharge was very long and mentally taxing. As we waited around for other people to do what they needed to do, see who they needed to see, talk to who they needed to talk to, sign and click the right buttons and boxes, I was reminded of the day I was discharged from the hospital after having our son. The difference was I was anxious to get home and start our new life with our brand-new baby. With Steve it was a lot of uncertainty. The amount of pain he was in…made me want to cry (just recalling his facial expressions, his moans, and the unknowns we knew lay ahead). However, thankfully everyone pulled through with their signoffs and Steve was discharged at 3:49 pm on Tuesday, October 11!

10-Day Challenge

We knew the next ten days were going to be a challenge since Steve would be dealing with pain management as his body built alternate channels to supply his leg and foot with ample blood supply. We were also hopeful that Steve being in the comforts of our home would yield him being able to sleep, his body to heal quickly and him getting back to his normal routine as soon as possible. He was worried about his job and wanting to feel well enough to get back to it. I tried to ease his mental chatter and tell him he needed to focus on his health, not a job, but in all honesty, I was concerned too. I wasn't sure if they'd hold the position for him – he played a big role in making sure people were taken care of and happy.

The week was pretty much a blur. I was getting up at 4 am, going to work, my days were filled with worry – both about Steve being at home in pain and making sure I was performing in my role with my new employer. I was off work at 2:30, so I was able to pick Talon up from school and get home to see how Steve had fared. I cooked dinner, help Talon with his homework, tried to maintain a sense of normalcy for the family, got Talon to bed, and the routine started all over again. The biggest difference was Steve was in so much pain that he camped out in our basement on the couch. When he would dangle his leg off the couch in just the right way it was able to provide just enough relief for him to fall asleep for a few moments.

In the summer before this whole ordeal started, we'd purchased tickets to Lantern Fest here in Denver. Steve and I agreed that Talon and I should go with our friends and try to have a night of normalcy. If you've never experienced a lantern festival, I highly recommend it. It's a Chinese tradition of setting a specific intention—be it letting go, reminiscing over a lost loved one, reaching a goal or whatever you desire. You think of that intention as you light a flame inside the lantern and release it into the air. Talon and I decorated the outside of our lantern with prayers and messages of hope for Steve. The experience was overwhelmingly magical and beautiful.

Seven days after he was released from the hospital, on Tuesday, October 18, Steve couldn't take it anymore, he begged me to take him back to the emergency department. His colorless face, and red, droopy eyes made sense as he described the pain to me. He said it was as if someone was holding a flame to his foot. When we pulled off his sock, I was mortified to see that his big toe was a deep purply-black.

Gangrene immediately popped in my head. Not that I knew much about it, but what I'd learned through television and movies I knew could be bad and potentially cause other health issues and even death. I quickly made another pleading phone call to our neighbor, Mr. Jerry, to see if they could take care of Talon for the evening.

The drive back to the emergency room for our third time was somber. My heart was heavy, I was scared and couldn't even wrap my brain around what Steve was going through. I was selfishly thinking about how I hated hospitals and the discomforts of his stay in ICU started flashing through my head as did all sorts of other outcomes. More than anything, I was worried that they were going to tell him that there was nothing they could do and send him home. I started playing out all these scenarios in my head and psyching myself up to fight for Steve.

Text to the family:
Date: Tuesday, October 18, 2016 at 4:42 PM
In route to Anschutz…

Pain on Top of Pain

One of the fellows who had assisted with a couple of Steve's surgeries got word that he was back in the emergency room and he came in to see what was going on. He was unable to find a pulse in his right foot and told him that he was going to be admitted back to the hospital for pain management. He briefly made mention that if the circulation in his foot didn't return soon, that he might be looking at an amputation of his foot.

My head was spinning as I tried to process this new potential outcome. I watched as they hooked my husband back up to a push button of Dilaudid, knowing that it wasn't going to touch the pain. So, I began researching. Looking for better medicine, types of amputations, mobility, complications, alternatives, you name it I was on the hunt for answers. One of the things I remember vividly was about phantom pain. My own interpretation: the longer Steve was in pain the longer his brain had time to make that a memory. Losing a limb, when in severe pain, could lock that painful memory into his brain. That would mean, he could still experience the same amount of pain with or without a foot.

The night was rough and restless. Like I suspected the Dilaudid did nothing for Steve's pain. He was able to push a button every ten minutes to administer more medication into his system and did just that. I watched him turn more and more into mush, except it was still painful. My night was filled with anything but sleep. I was swirling with emotions, thoughts, research, and worry. At this point I'm still super concerned that we haven't found a root cause of the kidney disease. Through my night of research, I did find something I thought might help with pain – a nerve block and some more thoughts about what might have caused the Minimal Change Disease. I started talking to the night nurse about the nerve block to see what she thought and by the early-morning rounds, now Wednesday, October 19, a vascular nurse we dealt with in ICU came by. I shared my thoughts with her and asked her every question I could think of about pain, amputations, and the kidney disease.

By mid-morning, an anesthesiologist put in a nerve block, unsure of what the actual plan is other than trying to control the pain enough to get Steve off the opioid medication and give his brain and body the rest it needed to heal and make decisions. The vascular nurse ordered a bunch of blood work in an effort to find the root cause of the kidney disease and arterial clotting. She also scheduled a podiatrist (foot doc) to come talk to us about a potential forefoot amputation. I made some phone calls, talked to a couple amputees, scheduled a prosthetist to come, and called my office to check in and let them know Steve was back in the hospital.

Text sent to update family:
Date: Wednesday, October 19, 2016 at 9:32 AM
Steve had a rough night, not much sleep. We still haven't seen a doc yet, but the vascular nurse we've dealt with came by. They just sent an anesthesiologist, who is doing a nerve block procedure right now. We're still not sure what the actual plan is yet, but they're hoping this will manage his pain enough to stop the opiate meds. We're also supposed to consult with the doc about what/when/how if they amputate. And we've asked to have blood work & possibly a colonoscopy while he's in here – just trying to find the root cause of his kidney disease & arterial clotting. They're

concerned that his pain will become permanent if they don't do this nerve block & there aren't any risks, so that's a plus. I'll send another update when we've spoken to the doc.

At this point although my new work family was trying to be supportive, I was starting to get questioned about my seemingly lack of help. "Where are Steve's parents? Can't they come to help you?" I explained that even if my in-laws came, there was no way I would be leaving Steve's side.

I didn't share this, but I was absolutely terrified that any moment could be the last. I wasn't getting answers from the medical personnel and wasn't confident that he wouldn't get another blood clot, or that his heart would be able to take all the drugs, pain, and trauma, or a plethora of other crazy-no sleep-worried wife thoughts.

And in all honesty, I didn't want my in-laws to come. They had been asking when they could come, but with us being in and out of the hospital it just didn't seem like the right time. I selfishly didn't want to have more on my plate to worry about. They weren't the type to fly in, rent a car and check into a hotel, and they hadn't spoken to my brother-in-law for the past two and a half to three months, so I felt them coming would be a burden on me.

Confused

Shortly after lunch the surgeon stopped by and left us with no real news. He said that he had exhausted everything he could do surgically and medically to improve Steve's condition. His suggestion was to get Steve back home, to fight through the pain, and hope that his body would build alternate channels to feed his foot ample blood supply. Steve asked what the doctor thought his chances were and how long it would take his body to produce channels. The surgeon's answer was less than ideal, "I can't say, 1% to 100%, three weeks to three months, we just don't know." His questioning tone made his response even worse than the words, but when he followed it with, "If it doesn't work and your toes start to turn black, we won't have a choice and we will have to amputate." The decision for the course of action was going to be totally up to Steve. In the meantime, the doctor suggested leaving in the nerve block for the night and reconvening tomorrow.

Text sent to update family:
Date: Wednesday, October 19, 2016 at 12:38 PM
Steve's surgeon just left…to be honest with no real news. He wants to leave the nerve block in for the night & reconvene tomorrow. The Dr said he's exhausted everything he can he can do surgically & medically to improve his condition. He said that he can go home & fight through the pain for 3 wks to 3 mon + totally leaving it up to Steve to decide…(they just don't know) in HOPES that his body will produce collaterals

or his toes will turn black & they'll HAVE to amputate. We could tell the Dr was totally leaving it up to Steve to decide.

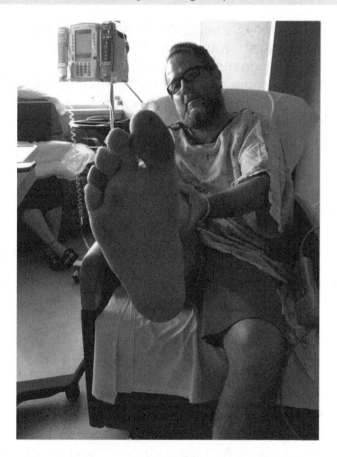

Over the next four hours, Steve and I talked a lot about his choices, how he was feeling, what he was thinking, and what I could do to help. None of it really prepared us for the conversation with the podiatrist who came just before 6:00. After examining Steve's foot, he concluded that his foot was dying. He wasn't comfortable with performing a forefoot amputation because he couldn't predict the integrity of the blood flow, knowing that the vascular surgeon was only able to open one artery down to Steve's ankle.

His theory, based off seeing the same type of thing happen time and time again, was that if Steve wanted to elect a forefoot amputation, he would probably end up coming back to cut off a little more, and then a little more, and it was possible that while trying to preserve as much of his body as possible he could end up losing the leg above the knee or even at the hip. The podiatrist said that if it was his body, he would elect to bypass all the pain and heartache and just elect to have a below-knee amputation.

Our hearts were heavy after hearing that news and we were confused. Steve's surgeon was telling him to go home for an unknown amount of time and try to deal with the pain for an unknown outcome, and the podiatrist was telling him that his foot is dying, to bypass a forefoot amputation and go straight for a below-knee amputation. Both of us were delirious with random thoughts, but eventually Steve fell asleep. I tried to sleep. I maybe managed to get 15 minutes here and there, but my mind was a mess.

Text sent to update family:
Date: Wednesday, October 19, 2016 at 5:43 PM
The podiatrist came & spoke with us this evening. He says that his foot is dying & in his opinion not worth trying to save. We will be speaking with the vascular team tomorrow morning regarding a lower leg amputation (based on where the blood flow stops). As you can imagine this is a hard decision, but we're confident in it and just as for your prayers for the road ahead.

Not 24 hours after the nerve block had been put in, Steve was in excruciating pain again. This was a pain he hadn't felt before. His foot was no longer swollen and had turned totally gray. The nurses on duty thought that something might be obstructed, but they discovered that Steve's body had rejected the never block – his body had literally pushed it out.

Thankfully, acute pain management was able to come within 30 minutes, but Steve was in such excruciating pain that it took four nurses to pin him down and keep him still enough for them to administer another nerve block. I watched his foot literally change colors in front of me, from gray-black to pink-red splotches. It took about 30 minutes for the bolus of the nerve block medication to kick in before Steve wasn't hurting anymore.

Text sent to update family:
Date: Thursday, October 20, 2016 at 7:15 AM
The Steve woke up at 5:30 this morning in excruciating pain…a pain that he hadn't felt before. His foot no longer is swollen & turned totally grey, so the nurses though something was obstructed. They verified this nerve block was in place & working. He went through about 30min of sheer pain before the bolus of nerve block kicked in. I've watched his foot change colors in front of me, from grey back to pink-red splotches. The vascular team should be in here any minute & I'll give another update then.

Keeping in mind that Steve was at a learning hospital, when the vascular team came by for their morning rounds, acute pain management joined them. They were all talking amongst themselves sharing their perspective and knowledge from their role within Steve's care. The only thing I think everyone agreed on is that Steve needed to remain pain-free for longer than 24 hours.

And then it happened! I completely lost it on the eight or nine people that were in the room, not in a mean or angry way, more like a heavy-hearted-but-I-totally-mean-business kind of way. I didn't feel that we were being properly communicated with. We hadn't heard anything about all the blood work and test results from the barrage of things Steve had done up to that point. Here my husband was, still fighting pain with no answers, and being faced with a decision that would affect the rest of his life.

Not to mention the mixed messages we were getting. One department would tell us one thing and another specialty would tell us something different. Steve was being encouraged by the vascular group to go home for at least a month to give his body time to build alternate channels of blood flow, and that if he had to amputate it would only be the forefoot. Due to the pain, they wanted to attempt to send him home with a nerve block, but he would have to go back to the hospital every other day to have it checked, cleaned and refilled. However, pain management told us they'd never done that before. The podiatrist told us that his foot was already dying and he didn't feel comfortable with a forefoot amputation.

Vascular agreed to get us all of the test results for us to see for ourselves. They tested him for everything under the sun and all looked normal. They were confident that this was all due to his Minimal Change Disease, his kidney leaking protein causing the blood clotting. The bad news was they still had no earthly idea what caused the Minimal Change Disease. And thanks to my barrage of questions, they also agreed that they, the vascular group, pain management, and podiatry would all come talk to us at the same time to make sure everyone was all on the same page.

Not long after the vascular group left, Steve's hematology team stopped by. They concurred that their tests weren't showing any other causes but agreed to get those test results to us too. They were also going to consult with another hematologist to get another set of eyes on the case and make sure they hadn't missed anything. In addition, just for peace of mind, they ordered an echocardiogram. The goal with that was to rule out a hole in his heart or additional clotting. Steve appeared as though he was comprehending what they were saying, but out of nowhere he started talking about being a superhero. The guys just looked at me, smiled, and without skipping a beat finished the conversation primarily making eye contact with me.

I told the guys Steve's delusional rendition of a superhero wasn't the first I'd seen of drug induced hysteria. Dilaudid was the drug I'd come to despise the most. Or perhaps it was the combination of the Dilaudid and Oxycodone. Either way it wasn't good and was clearly turning Steve's brain to mush. The long-term effects were looming in the back of my mind, but there was so much more to focus on.

Text sent to update family:
Date: Thursday, October 20, 2016 at 10:51 AM
6 people from vascular came to see Steve this morning (acute pain management is here now). Vascular wants Steve to be pain-free to be able to make the best decision possible. I lost it on them a little this morning & told them we're not getting proper communication. He's being expected to make this life altering decision & we're still unclear of the cause. They are getting us ALL the test results for us to see for ourselves, but they've tested him for everything & all looks normal. They're confident that this is all due to his Minimal

Change Disease (kidney) leaking protein & his natural anticoagulant & that nothing else has cause the MCD.

I also just spoke to the hematologist who said the same thing – no other causes & he's getting us their test results. In addition, he's consulting a third hemo Dr to look at Steve's case to make sure they haven't missed anything. And they will come back again today.

In addition, they're ordered one last thing, in their opinion, JUST for peace of mind… an echocardiogram. This will rule out a hole in his heart or additional clotting. His vascular surgeon will also come by today.

Please pray for controlled pain until Steve finalizes his decision & they get him into surgery. His chances of phantom pain increases dramatically if he's in pain when they amputate.

Chop it Off!

What a blessing that the second nerve block attempt was successful and Steve was able to sleep for a solid 4 hours. A physical medicine specialist stopped by and explained what to expect between the two amputations – forefoot and below knee. By the time Steve's vascular surgeon from ICU came to chat, we were both mentally exhausted. We'd had a lot of interaction and I think both of us were trying to process all the different scenarios. However, when the surgeon started to lecture Steve about needing to go home with the nerve block and ride it out, I interjected by asking him to step outside the room.

Out in the hallway I told the surgeon that he was being unreasonable and making Steve feel guilty. I told him that if Steve decided to amputate that we didn't think that meant he, as Steve's surgeon, failed us. In fact, I shared that Steve and I were both appreciative of everything he had done. We thought he was to thank for this being a decision between riding out the pain or amputating. I looked him in the eyes and said that I know he told me in ICU that this would never be an amputation situation, but if that's what Steve decided then that's okay. I encouraged him to go back in the room and tell Steve that whatever he decided was the right decision for him, and that's exactly what he did.

Texts sent to update family:
Date: Thursday, October 20, 2016 at 7:43 PM
It's been a busy day with lots of conversation with really no decision or direction. Steve's been battling pain all day, even

with the nerve block in place. They're encouraging him to go home for a month+ to give his body time to build collaterals for a change to only have to amputate from the forefoot down vs just below knee down. However, not sure that Steve can endure his pain for another month, plus there are reasons why that could be bad. Of course he wants to save what he can, but he's faced with quality of life decisions & it's just hard.

We've also been given mixed messages/info so tomorrow vascular, pain mgmt., & podiatry will come talk to us at the same time to make sure we're all on the same page.

Date: Friday, October 21, 2016 at 9:25 AM
Acute pain is finally here to replace Steve's nerve block catheter (it came out last night & he's been battling pain the whole time). This will provide him another 18-24 hours of (hopefully) 0 pain. When it wears off he'll be able to tell if the new meds that will continue to drip through the catheter will work & therefore if he can foresee going home to "deal" with the pain for a month.

Date: Friday, October 21, 2016 at 4:53 PM
The nerve block was successful & Steve slept for 4 hours. He saw a physical medicine specialist, who discussed the expectation between the 2 amputations. His surgeon told us that whichever decision Steve makes is the right decision. He talked to an amputee who laid out some of his trials, thoughts, etc. We're hoping to see a prosthesis, who will be able to give him a low down on what kind of prosthetic they'd be able to give him.

Hallelujah, it's Saturday, October 22, and the nerve block was still working! Which was amazing news because I knew there was much to be done. When you're looking for a new vehicle you talk to people, you do research, you go look at and even give them a test drive. Well, that's kind of how we treated this decision. What kind of prosthetic would he have, what colors, shoes, hardware, software, size, shape...? You name it, we tried to think of every possible question we could. Think about it, this is going to be your mode of transportation for the rest of your life - you want to make the right decision. Not like you can just trade it in!

We talked to a prosthetist who shared what Steve could expect as well as how things work. We were also able to speak with two below-knee amputees. One of the amputee's was a phone call with a gentleman that my parents went to church with. The other came to visit us at the hospital. While their amputation stories varied, the common denominator was mental awareness and strength. They were both transparent with how hard this would be and how much Steve's life would change, but they were also inspirational and gave him hope for a positive outcome if he went into it with some mental preparation. To be honest, I'm not sure you can actually mentally prepare for having your leg chopped off any more than you can prepare for the death of a loved one who's ill. It's still a loss and something that takes time to heal from - mentally and physically in this case.

At some point that afternoon Steve asked me what he was doing, what the hang up was, and why the doctors hadn't scheduled the amputation yet. "Oh dear," I thought to myself. I took a deep breath and told him that the doctors were waiting for HIM to make a decision. By this point I was more than aware that the drugs had really done a number on his brain, but I couldn't imagine how he didn't know why he was just sitting in the hospital. "What do you mean, why would they be waiting for me?" he asked genuinely and thoroughly confused. "Well, because you have options. You can go home with or without the nerve block, and potentially suffer through more pain in hopes that your body will build alternate channels to feed your foot the blood supply it needs. You can elect for a forefoot amputation, or you can choose a below-knee amputation. The doctors aren't going to make the choice for you, the decision is yours and they're waiting for you to make it." I sighed to myself and waited for that information to sink in.

To my surprise he quickly responded, "I can't deal with this pain anymore, and the foot doc said he wouldn't do an amputation, so I only have one choice." I slowly got up from the couch and walked over to stand in front of him. He was sitting in a recliner chair right next to the hospital bed. "Okay, so the next time the doctors come in, you have to tell them. I mean you have to physically say, out loud, what you want them to do." I grabbed his hand and gazed into his eyes, "Can you say it, out loud? I think you need to practice by telling me." He squeezed my hand tightly and with tears welling up in his eyes he said, "I want a below-knee amputation." Oh, how those words cut. I leaned over, engulfed him in a hug, and we cried together for a moment.

Text sent to update family:
Date: Saturday, October 22, 2016 at 1:14 PM
Steve's nerve block is still working! He's seen a prosthetist & amputee today. He made his decision, he's going to do a below knee amputation. We don't have any other info right now, but I'll send another update when we do. Visitors are welcome!

The rest of the afternoon and evening consisted of several visitors both friends and family. There was a lot of laughter and joking around by everyone. It felt almost normal. I had also gotten a call from one of Steve's buddy's that he served in the Navy with. He suggested that I file with Veterans Affairs for insurance. He went on to tell me that he'd heard that amputees in the civilian world have a lot of red tape and restrictions with what they can get and when they can get it. I'd also read articles to that effect. Meanwhile, helping amputees was one of the best things that the military did. I hadn't even considered the VA, but I figured we had nothing to lose. So in between visitors I spent time filling out the application and getting everything submitted.

During the morning rounds on Sunday, October 23, the vascular surgeon and an entourage of five other doctors and medical students walked in. Steve almost nonchalantly declared "Chop it off!" They, of course, made him clarify and talked for a bit, sharing a little bit of Steve's journey, so far, to the medical students.

Text sent to update family:
Date: Sunday, October 23, 2016 at 10:19 AM
Steve's surgery will be tomorrow, probably in the afternoon. We will have a better time after rounds tomorrow morning.

The Amputation

After telling Steve's parents, who I'd been in communication with daily, they decided they needed to come. Since they weren't going to make it in time for the amputation surgery, and I knew the added stress it would cause, I asked them to wait until Thanksgiving. I thought it would be best to give us a few weeks to figure things out and have something to look forward to and celebrate together. My suggestion was ignored as I got a text that they had booked their flight and would be arriving in Denver that Thursday evening.

If you were to get to know Steve, he's super blunt, sarcastic, witty and downright funny. When I shared the news about the amputation with our friends and family, most of them were in shock and clearly didn't know the right thing to say. However, some of our closest friends called me later that day and asked if they could bring us dinner and throw Steve a farewell to his leg party.

They surprised us with a pirate-themed cake that dawned the words, "Sorry about your leg Matey!" They brought Steve an eye patch and parrot and the only thing he needed to complete the pirate look was a peg leg. Tee-hee!

They snuck in a couple beers and brought a couple more friends with them. It was a small "party," but we enjoyed our dinner, cake and some laughs, which took our minds off of what the next day would bring. In case you're wondering, the nurses on the floor thought it was great. Several of them stopped by the room, even ones that we hadn't yet met.

They were impressed by Steve's positivity and demeanor hearing all he'd been through and what he was facing.

October 24, 2016 at 5:03 pm they took Steve down to surgery. The amputation took just over two and a half hours and they allowed me to meet him in the post-op area right after waking him up. My heart was pounding as I peered around the corner not knowing what to expect. He was sitting up, bandaged leg out in plain sight, and he was chatting away with the nurse. I was shocked by his attitude. I mean I didn't want him to be depressed, sad, or in pain, but I honestly expected it. He was in such high spirits. Like, unusually high spirits. I asked him how he was doing, and he smiled, looked down and said, "Well, it's gone. FINALLY!" I guess that's what happens when you've been in such acute pain - just relieved that the pain was over and he was ready to start this new chapter in his life.

My parents were waiting for us when we got back to the room. The nurse wasn't able to help Steve get from one bed to the other, so as she started to go get help, he just moved himself over. I felt like all the oxygen was taken from the room with all of the gasps. That's my man! I thought. Confident, independent and just doing what needed to be done. We visited with my parents for a bit and when they left Steve and I were both exhausted. The emotional drain and knowing he was out of pain lead to the most sleep I'd gotten in the hospital. I think the same was true for Steve too.

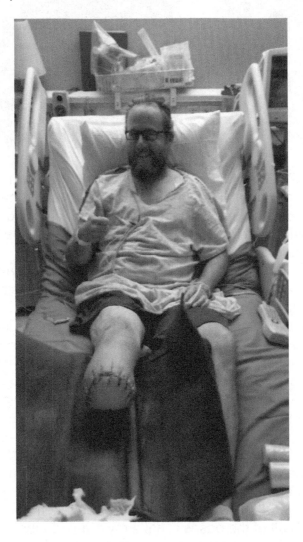

There was no rest; the day after the amputation Steve had physical therapy twice. They were figuring out what his preference was for temporary mobility; regular or forearm crutches, plus ensuring that he was able to use them with ease. He struggled with surgical and phantom pains throughout the day, but it was nothing compared to what he'd been dealing with. His brother brought his laptop to the hospital, and they watched Cleveland take the lead over the Cubs in Game 1 of the World Series.

 Danette Penrod is 😊 feeling loved.
October 25, 2016 · 👥

Day after his below the knee amputation...PT knocked out twice, handling the surgical & phantom pains in stride & now watching his Cubbies! Thank you all for your prayers, well wishes, friendship & support.

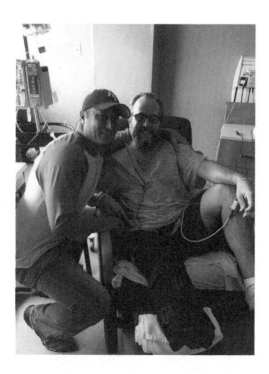

The next few days were more of the same. More physical therapy, shifting him over to pills versus the IV drips, getting him slowly disconnected from all the monitors, and making sure he was prepared for his release. Steve was anxiously ready to get home, which finally happened, Thursday, October 27.

Returning Home

Pulling into the driveway was a bit surreal. Neither of us had seen our son much in the past month. I was looking forward to being a family again and getting accustomed to our new normal. Not 30 minutes after we got home, Steve's brother Scott pulled up, dropping off their parents who had just got into town. I could feel how gut wrenching it was for them to see their son for the first time, missing part of his body. It was nice to catch up and we talked through some of the upcoming challenges Steve would be facing. We also discussed what we would need to do to our home to ensure his safety and utmost comfort with a sense of normalcy. It felt good to start verbalizing things out loud. After all, this whole situation was new to us! There was no way we could fully comprehend all that we were going to go through.

Sleeping in our bed, together, for the first time in well over a month was wonderful and weird at the same time. I was worried about tossing and turning and kicking the freshly amputated leg. We got through it and Steve had a good night's rest. I hadn't been sleeping well since this all started, so it was no surprise that I was up every hour and my thoughts were racing all over creation.

The next morning Steve decided that his hair and beard had gotten a bit unruly, having been unattended to for so long. He wasn't up for trying to balance on one leg to shave, so he decided to try a barber where they would take care of him for both needs. He asked his dad if he wanted to go with him, and he said no. I asked my mother-in-law if she wanted to go with me to drop him off and do a little retail therapy while we waited, and she said no. I was a little taken aback that neither of them wanted to go, but off we went, while they stayed behind and hung out with Talon. Steve was adamant that he just wanted me to drop him off at the curb. So that's just what I did. I hung out in the area and waited for him to call me to tell me he was finished. As I pulled back up, he looked so good, but I got a little choked up as I realized the forearm crutches and amputated leg.

 Danette Penrod is 😌 thanking God. ...
October 28, 2016 · 👥

Can't even begin to express our gratitude for our family & friends. Your emotional support, love, and prayers has kept us a float. We're so thankful and blessed that Steve is home and that his situation wasn't more severe.

When we got home, I asked my mother-in-law to take a family photo so I could send out an update to everyone and include a picture. Not long after I was dinking around in the kitchen and cleaning up after lunch when I heard Steve say in a booming voice, "What did you just say to me?" As I peered into the living room, I could see flames coming off Steve's head. His dad repeated, "It's time for you to grow up and be a man!" Steve and his dad started yelling at one another so I ran into the room and shouted "Enough! I will not tolerate negativity in this house!" My father-in-law got up and went down to the basement. I looked at my mother-in-law and said, "You have to fix this." And with that she took off for the basement.

"What in the world?" I asked Steve. He told me that they were just talking and out of nowhere his dad told him he needed to grow up and be a man. In hindsight, this more than likely started out as normal bantering about Steve's chin hair – something his dad always did was question and tease him about his facial hair. I assume it escalated with all the crazy mixed emotions and was blown way out of proportion. First, his dad shouldn't have ever let Steve's facial hair cause him to say such an outlandish comment, and secondly, Steve wasn't in the right frame of mind, having just endured seemingly endless pain, surgery after surgery, and an amputation, to accept the razzing. I was honestly surprised that Steve didn't kick his parents out of the house, it was that bad.

The day went on and Steve's parents stayed in the basement all day. Steve hung out on the couch, rested and watched television. I hadn't really been home for any length of time in a month, so I decided to clean. As dinner rolled around, I hollered a couple questions down to my in-laws, but that was the extent of the communication. We managed to eat dinner together in silence except for the background noise that was on TV. It was so uncomfortable that I decided to head to bed early. I hugged my in-law's goodnight and told them I loved them as I retreated upstairs. Steve came up not long after and said that neither of his parents had gotten up to hug him and didn't respond when he said, "I love you, goodnight." I couldn't imagine what he must have felt in the moment and my heart sank. I hugged him and told him he was loved deeply.

The next morning, we went out to breakfast with Steve's folks and we all pretended that everything was okay. In fact, we didn't talk about the incident from the previous day at all. Thank goodness for kids. I felt like Talon was a buffer for the whole day. Early that evening, Steve's aunt, uncle, brother Scott & Scott's family came over for dinner. It was a nice reprieve from the awkwardness and tension we'd been suffering through. My entertainment skills that evening consisted of pizza, served on paper plates (and I'm not even sure I ordered the pizza).

Steve's parents loved breakfast, and we were fortunate enough to have a Village Inn right across the street, so Sunday morning (October 30) we went out to breakfast again. The whole day was like déjà vu, pretending like everything was okay. I did talk to my mother-in-law to question why there hadn't been an apology, but there wasn't much said to shed any light on how they were feeling or if an apology would be coming. Later that afternoon, we went over to Scott and Kara's to hang out and have dinner. They graciously offered to host, knowing it would be easier on me, plus their house was more accommodating for the six adults and three kids. It was also a huge gesture since Scott hadn't spoken to his parents in four months, since their fight in June. Not only did he set that aside and pick them up from the airport, but he and his family had joined us the previous night for dinner and welcomed them into their home so we could all be together as a family.

Unfortunately, the tension didn't get any better over at their house. In fact, things got a little worse. One of Scott's buddy's, Casey, that we knew, was at their house when we arrived. He wanted to see Steve in person and give him a hug. Introductions were made to Steve's parents and all was fine until Casey's wife showed up a little while later with their son who'd been napping. Kara was busy in the kitchen cooking and glanced up and gestured to Jon and Carla that Casey's wife belonged to him. As people started talking, I noticed that my in-laws had retreated to the couch away from everyone and were whispering. I just let it go and focused on enjoying my time with family and friends. Casey and his wife only stayed for a little while and left before dinner, but Steve's parents still seemed distant.

After dinner we all retreated to the living room to get comfortable and chat. Steve was sitting on the couch when he suddenly started having muscle cramps and shooting nerve pain. He took off his protective sleeve to try to massage it, but that yielded no help. It was super scary for all of us to witness and what made it worse was he was unable to straighten his knee to get the protective sleeve back on. It was getting late, so we decided to drive the 20 minutes home, get Talon to bed, and get Steve's pain medication. After over an hour of solid pain, Steve and I agreed that he needed to go back to the hospital – I think we were both beyond scared and had no idea what in the world was going on. Steve's mom asked if they could go with us, but I deflected by telling her that I really needed them to stay home with Talon, plus they were flying out early the next morning.

Another Hospital Stay

Little did I know that Steve would be admitted back to the hospital to begin treatment for an infection and for pain management, although we weren't clear if he truly had an infection or not. The ultrasound and CT scans didn't show anything. They took blood cultures in the emergency department but told us it would take 72 hours before they could determine if there was an infection. The vascular team wasn't concerned with an infection. Steve's residual limb had a little swelling and redness, but that was deemed normal, so their primary focus was to get Steve out of pain and for him to be able to straighten his knee.

Sadly, nothing stopped his pain. After the shot of Morphine didn't work, they gave him a bolus of Dilaudid. When that did nothing, they gave him a 10-minute PCA of Dilaudid (that's a push button, where he could self-administer the drug every 10 minutes). And that did nothing either, so on top of all of it he was given 30mg of Oxycodone, which was repeated every 4 hours.

At this point I'm freaking out inside. I'm super concerned because they can't figure out why he's in so much pain or how to get it under control. The number of drugs that are being pumped into his body seems excessive, especially since they aren't doing anything. My head was a whirlwind of thoughts. Thinking about worst case scenarios, how this will affect Talon in the morning, what his parents are going to do, having to go to work, how to share this news with family and friends, how long will Steve be in the hospital, what am I going to do about Halloween for Talon...on and on my thoughts raced out of control.

I left the hospital around 3 am to go home, take a power nap, shower, and head into work. I was only able to sleep for about an hour before my alarm went off. After getting ready, my mother-in-law greeted me and we talked for a few minutes before I headed out the door for work. I had arranged for our neighbor, Jerry, to come over and stay with Talon to get him off to school after my in-laws left for the airport.

Text sent to update family:
Date: Tuesday, October 31, 2016 at 7:31 AM
Steve was admitted back at Anschutz University last night. He was he was having a lot of pain – muscle cramps & shooting nerve pain. ER was treating him for an infection, but his vascular team isn't concerned. His CT scan & Ultrasound came back normal. He has some swelling & redness in his remaining limb, but said that's normal – they're still giving him antibiotics & focusing on trying to get him back out of the hospital (NOT tonight). We're not understanding what's going on. Please pray for healing, no pain, answers & peace of mind.

My workday felt long as I was anxious to get back to the hospital. Thankfully because I went into work so early, it also meant I got off at 2:30, so by 3:00 I was back at the hospital. Nothing had changed in the last 12 hours. He was still in pain, couldn't straighten his knee, and was left without answers. I understood there was family tension but was shocked to learn that my in-laws didn't change their flight or even stop by the hospital to visit Steve before they flew out.

I struggled to suppress the anger I felt with Steve's situation, being back in the hospital. I knew the only way he'd be able to be released from the hospital was to not be hooked up to machines, and he was still connected to push button of Dilaudid. I knew he needed to straighten his leg out, and soon, or he may never be able to wear a prosthetic. It was a frightening situation and I didn't feel my husband was of sound mind to comprehend the ramifications of his decisions. I tried to have a heart-to-heart conversation with him, but he was so bitter. I felt like he was blaming me for him being back in the hospital again.

Drugs

Drugs had been a huge topic of conversation for us both in and out of the hospital. The laundry list of things Steve was on coming home from the hospital was mind blowing to me. 60mg of Prednisone, the steroid he'd been on since September to treat the Minimal Change Disease in his kidneys. Protonix was recommended to take along with the Prednisone to treat potential acid reflux. He was prescribed two different doses of Flexeril, a muscle relaxant, 5mg twice during the day and 10mg to take a bedtime. Warfarin, a blood thinner that requires regular and careful INR (international normalized ratio) checks via hospital blood draws. 81mg low dose Aspirin, for combatting arterial clotting. Colace, was an optional prescription, along with MiraLAX to help with constipation. 600mg Gabapentin 3x/day, used to treat nerve pain, and prescribed to help specifically with phantom pain. Cleocin, to help treat a wide variety of bacterial infections. Enoxaparin (syringe injections) used to prevent blood clots in the blood vessels of the legs. And the one I dreaded the most, 30mg Oxycodone 6x/day, an opioid used to treat severe pain.

I set everything out and labeled them with the description and times he was supposed to take them. When I was home I made sure I was on top of them, and when I was at work, I had timers set to send him a text to remind him. We'd had several arguments about the drugs. He was prescribed and taking drugs that were highly addictive. Problem was they weren't working, so I couldn't comprehend him staying on them. He couldn't fathom not taking them because, well, he'd just had his leg amputated and it's what the doctors told him he needed.

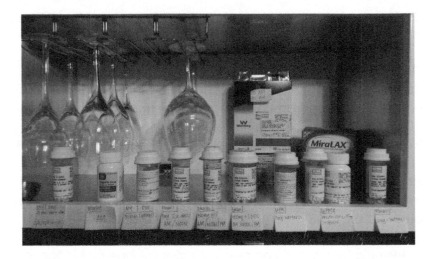

We'd had several different doctors and nurses suggest that the pain he was in this time around was due to him starting to step down off his Oxy too soon. Four days after the amputation, in preparation for him going home, the doctors had lowered him from 30mg to 25mg, taking it every 4 hours. Four days later we decided to reduce his intake from 25mg to 20mg, still taking it every 4 hours. While I understand that you're supposed to stay ahead of the pain with Oxycodone, the notion that he was back in the hospital due to only being on 20mg of Oxy made no sense to me. Morphine and Dilaudid weren't touching the pain and they'd put him back on 30mg of Oxycodone every 4 hours with no change to his pain level or mobility in straightening his leg.

As Steve's bitterness grew about being back in the hospital and being back in pain even after his leg was gone, his attitude towards me was awful and the professionals were feeding him with what I felt was misinformation. I think they were just throwing out what sounded like a good answer, him stepping down off the Oxy too soon, when in reality they had no idea why he was back in the hospital in pain.

I pushed back my anger and frustration and from sheer compassion, shared my thoughts about what he needed to do to be released. I'm not sure if it was his resentment towards me or him just being a tuff guy, but I felt as though my thoughts were dismissed without any regard. Inside I was starting to give up. I didn't know what else to say or do, which fueled my irritation.

About the time I'd exhausted my efforts, Steve got a visit from a physical therapist. I swear to you, she nearly verbatim told him what I had just said. He looked at me with annoyance to which I responded, "I've never met or spoken to her in my life." I quickly turned to her and thanked her, telling her that we had literally just had the same conversation. So, with that, Steve decided to dig deep and get his leg stretched out.

As soon as his leg was fairly straight, blood started gushing out. I ran out to grab a nurse and when we came back into the room it looked like a murder had taken place, no joke. It wasn't any more painful than it had been, so with the nurse's consent, Steve continued to work on keeping his knee straight. The nurse got things cleaned up as I just sat and watched Steve with such hope in his eyes.

I think it's important to note here that I'm convinced Steve's admittance back into the hospital this time had little/nothing to do with lowering his dose of Oxy. I felt Steve was back in the hospital because of all the family stress and drama that had transpired the past few days. Now that we've lived through it, I know those thoughts to be true.

The Fall

Steve had always taken Talon out trick-or-treating. Some friends of ours had invited him over to go out with their boys, but Steve and I agreed that I should go home earlier that night to join the festivities. To be honest, all I wanted to do was go home and crawl into bed. Other than my hour nap, I'd been up for 34 hours. When I arrived at our friends, I joked that there was no costume needed – I looked horrible and was a zombie-mom. We had a wonderful time despite knowing Steve was in the hospital alone and I showered him with pictures trying to keep his mind occupied on all the reasons to come home.

Those three days and three nights felt like time stood still. I kept an awful schedule. Up at 4 am, work till 2:30, at the hospital from 3-8:30 pm, and home in time to give Talon a kiss as he went to bed. My mind kept stirring, but I would eventually fall asleep out of exhaustion somewhere between 10-10:30 pm and the whole process would start over again. Although we had wonderful friends and family who were helping us with Talon, I truly felt like I had abandoned our nine-year-old, and that weighed heavily on me all while trying to be there for my husband and manage my new job.

The statements from the professionals about Steve's pain returning because of the lack of Oxycodone really took a toll on him and that led to us having some pretty heated conversations. I was also catching grief from the doctors, and we argued about dosing and drug choices. I had no apologies, no one was around for the drug comas, delusional episodes, and didn't know Steve well enough to understand the level of brain fog he had. I was legitimately concerned with the long-term effects that Steve might experience, and I was going to advocate for him even if he felt otherwise. Thankfully the one thing the doctors and I agreed on was getting him back home, so they stopped the intravenous drugs and gave him instructions on what he had to do to get the green light to be released.

When the physical therapy department knew he was ready to work and get released, they came and observed him and gave the thumbs up that he could go home. By Wednesday evening (11/2), a little after 6pm, though he was still in pain, it was becoming a little more manageable and he was released.

The release couldn't have come at a better time. Game 7 of the World Series was about to start. After arriving home, we ate dinner as a family and it felt so good. Despite my better instincts, Steve wanted to watch the Cubs win the World Series on our big screen, so he went downstairs to our basement to watch the game. There ended up being a long rain delay, so I retreated to bed around 9:30. Just after 1 am I woke up to a crashing sound. I ran into the kitchen to find Steve laying on the floor. "Are you okay? What in the world happened?" I said with a panic-ridden streak in my voice. Apparently in his exhaustion, Steve didn't lift the crutches high enough on the last step and fell forward landing all his weight on his residual limb.

I sat on the floor next to him, tears started to well up in both our eyes. We were so scared. He couldn't fathom having to go back to the hospital. I asked what he was feeling and told him I thought we needed to look at the wound. We were both fighting back our emotions as I removed the protective sleeve. No blood. I slowly removed the bandages to reveal a swollen and red wound, but all the stitches and staples were in place and there was no blood or indication that he'd done any damage. I think the sigh of relief we both released could've been heard by our neighbors. I got him rebandaged, his protective sleeve put back on, and helped him off the floor. I crawled back into bed and just cried myself back to sleep.

Danette Penrod
November 4, 2016 · 👥   ···

Shout out to all the amazing doctors, nurses & surgeons at University of Colorado Medical Campus. Thank you for your professionalism, knowledge & friendliness. May Steve never be your patient again!

The next three weeks were awkward at best. Steve trying to manage the pain, heal, and mentally adjust to his new reality. Me running a vicious cycle of trying to manage a work-home life balance with the added responsibility of managing appointments, pills, and playing nurse. I continued to enlist the help of friends and family to help get Steve to his plethora of appointments. Talon's teacher was so sweet, she had a son the same age, so she would pick Talon up on her way to school and the boys would hang out together until school started.

The best news we received during that time was that Steve's kidneys were no longer leaking protein - the Minimal Change Disease was "cleared" and on November 15, he began stepping down off the steroid.

Holey Bleeding

On Tuesday, November 29, Steve had an appointment to have his staples and stitches removed. We were both very excited about this appointment because it meant healing and getting closer to being able to walk. When I got home from work I ran very excitedly into our living room, I couldn't wait to see! As he unwrapped his residual limb I started seeing blood. To my horror, as the last piece of the bandage was removed, he literally had holes where the staples had been removed. They left in the stitches as it was the only thing keeping him closed, but he was bleeding out from every opening. I ran and grabbed Helichrysum essential oil. I knew it helped naturally clot blood, as it had worked wonders with Talon's nose bleeds – the main reason I'd purchased it. I gently cleaned his skin the best I could and applied the essential oil to the clean skin just above the holes. Before I added the new bandage to wrap him back up, I added a couple drops of oil so the wound would be able to marinate with it.

The next morning (November 30), when Steve woke up, he called me at work to tell me he'd woken up with a fever and had pain in his bone just below his knee. Terrified of an infection, I told him to really pay attention to his body and if he started feeling any worse, he needed to get back to the hospital. He gradually started to feel better as the day went on and by the time I got home, he was feeling pretty good, no pain to speak of and no fever.

When I changed out his dressing there were only a couple holes dripping blood. Although that was better than the day before we were still concerned about an infection. Still confused why they'd sent him home like that, we took pictures and sent them to his prosthetist to see what his thoughts were. As we waited for a reply, I cleaned the wounds and applied more of the Helichrysum just above the gaping holes, put a few drops of oil on the new bandage and got it rewrapped. Just about that time the prosthetist called and was furious. He couldn't believe what he was looking at and told us that was not normal.

Steve didn't have any problems, no pain or fever, the rest of the evening or next day. However, when I got home from work late that afternoon, now Thursday, December 1, Steve's prosthetist came to visit because he wanted to see the open wounds in person. He was mortified. He took new pictures and sent a write-up to the hospital. Later that evening the vascular nurse called Steve and scheduled him an appointment to come in the next morning so they could have a look at it.

God bless our neighbor, Jerry. He had been such a blessing to us in helping with Talon when Steve was in and out of the hospital, and now I was asking if he could help me get Steve to and from appointments. I called him to ask and thankfully Jerry was available to take Steve to his appointment that next morning. At this moment I'm feeling a lot. I'm super irritated at the situation. I'm in disbelief. I'm feeling guilty that I can't take Steve to the appointment and annoyed because I want to so I can question them and share my distaste for them sending him home with open wounds. I'm scared of the unknown. I'm disappointed in the vascular team, and I'm trying to feel through all of these emotions while trying to remain a calm and positive beacon for my man.

I got a call from Steve mid-morning saying he was being admitted back to hospital for another surgery. "What in the world are you talking about? What surgery?" My voice cracked as he explained that during the check-up they discovered some clotting and since he'd lost his leg due to a blood clot, they didn't want to take any chances. They wanted to open him back up, washout the clots and ensure that there was no infection. "Well, yeah you have clotting, I used Helichrysum oil to help you clot so you wouldn't bleed out, remember?" Then all the sudden I started to panic, had I done something wrong, did I hurt my man, was he having another surgery because of me? Steve recaptured my attention as he began explaining that they were able to stick a cotton swab several inches into one of the holes and they said that's a good indicator of an infection. If the infection had spread to the bone then they would have to amputate more. We knew that meant bad news for the prosthetic; his residual limb was at an ideal length. Plus, we didn't know if that meant going above the knee or what was going to happen.

Text sent to update family:
Date: Friday, December 2, 2016 at 10:12 AM
I just got off the phone with Steve. He's being admitted back into the hospital right now. He has to have another surgery (hopefully today) to clean out an infection. We're concerned that it's spread to his bone – if so they'll have to cut more off…VERY bad news for the prosthetic, not to mention this means starting over again in the healing department. Prayers are needed please!

I asked him what the plan was, so I knew what I needed to do about leaving work. They were hopeful to get him in that day but didn't have a plan. He told me he would call once they had a plan. After I hung up, I just sat there for a minute.

Could this really be happening? I grabbed my phone and sent a text to update everybody. Then decided to share with one of my bosses. As I stepped into the doorway of his office, he looked up at me and acknowledged with a head nod that it was okay to come in. I started crying. This boss was like the loving, caring dad of the office. His gentle eyes and sweet demeanor caused my emotional walls to feel comfortable enough to crumble in that moment. I was a mess of emotions. Guilt. Fear. Disappointment. Frustration. Sadness. Anger. This list goes on.

I started to explain the newest development in our situation, my boss looked mortified, and with tears in his eyes he told me how sorry he was. He couldn't imagine having to go through this and, of course, I could go or do anything I needed to do. His compassion was overwhelming.

My tears stopped in an instant, as if I'd turned off a tiny faucet. I went into game mode as I gathered my belongings to be ready for the call that I needed to leave but kept working. My guilt of all the work I'd already missed was coupled with my need for some normalcy in this moment. I figured it was Friday and if I could get through my workday that would be good for them and for me. Plus, I knew there was nothing I could do at the hospital but sit and wait for them to give Steve a time for what was going to be his sixth surgery.

Washout Surgery

I was relieved when no call came before my workday ended. I had already asked family to help me with Talon as I headed back to the hospital with such a heavy heart. It was just after 4:00, on December 2, when they were finally able to get him into surgery. This time around they decided the best way for him to heal would be to have a vacuum-assisted closure. That meant they didn't close him up with stitches or staples. They left the wound open, sticking a sponge in the opening and taping it closed with special tape and a vacuum hose attached. A wound VAC is designed to regulate the air pressure, gently pull fluid from the wound and reduce the chances of swelling and bacteria while stimulating new tissue growth to help the wound heal more quickly.

There was no visible infection, but they sent cultures to the lab to ensure their findings. They said that he had lots of clotting, both old and new blood and his wound wouldn't have healed in that state. The wound vacuum dressing has to be changed out every two days, so his release from the hospital was contingent on them getting him set up with a machine that he can take home and ensuring that a home care specialist was scheduled for the next couple weeks.

Text sent to update family:
Date: Friday, December 2, 2016 at 5:17 PM
Steve just got out of surgery. No visible infection, they'll send cultures to the lab. He had lots of clotting (old & new blood), so his wound wouldn't have healed in that state. They go him cleaned out & a wound vacuum put on. It will have to be changed our every 2 days. He won't go home until Mon/Tues & they'll set up home care to come change the dressing.

Because his surgery was done on a Friday night, he ended up having to spend the entire weekend in the hospital. The hospital scene was getting rather old at this point, but the big difference with this last surgery and stay was that Steve wasn't drugged up and he wasn't in pain. My phone had stopped working, and Steve was feeling fine, so I left in time to get to spend a little bit of time with Talon before he wanted to go to bed.

Saturday morning, I went and got a new phone. The store associate told me I had essentially broken it with all the text messages. I guess me keeping people up to date over the past couple months was too much for it to handle. If technology can just break down with all that stress, imagine what my brain was like. As a bonus, my new phone purchase also came with some free VR Gear. Talon and I couldn't wait to get to the hospital and try it!

My parents decided to take Talon home early in the evening on Saturday, so Steve and I could have a date night right there in the hospital room. The hospital was situated near a couple of Popeyes. Since we both love their spicy chicken but rarely get it, I thought it would be a treat to go get some and bring it back to the room. We enjoyed one another's company and every delicious bite. The rest of the weekend we spent time as a family in the hospital, playing with my new phone, using the virtual reality, and trying to make the most of a cruddy situation.

Despite my efforts to be optimistic with the situation, on at least two different occasions I had become so frustrated with Steve's treatment, or sometimes lack of, that I requested a patient advocate. There was an obvious lack of planning, staff and communication over the weekend. When the patient advocate finally came to see us late Sunday, I hate to admit it, their lack of knowledge, empathy and suggestions was mind boggling. They were worthless and of no help in trying to get Steve released.

A guy from hematology showed up not too long after and we talked to him in depth. He was one of the only people who'd been with Steve over the past few months that seemed genuinely fascinated with his story and wanted to help us get answers. He understood that the amputation wasn't necessary had we been taken seriously and listened to at our initial emergency room visit. He understood that we still had no answers as to why Steve had gotten Minimal Change Disease. And that our lives were forever changed without any real answers to the culprit.

Texts sent to update family:
Date: Monday, December 5, 2016 at 2:02 PM
Steve just had the wound vac dressing change. It's gone down about 30% since Fri night, so that's good. Still working on getting him released today, they haven't even started the process with the home wound care people. Sigh!

Date: Monday, December 5, 2016 at 5:14 PM
Well, it was too late in the day to get a wound vac – so it's a no go on going home.

Eventually the stars aligned. They were able to procure a wound vac that could leave the hospital, home care services were scheduled to come three times per week to change the wound vac dressing, appointments were made for hospital check-ins once a week through the end of the year, and Steve was finally cleared and released from the hospital late afternoon on Tuesday, December 6.

Wound Vac Life

That first night at home [again], going to bed was ... interesting. We had to hang the wound vac machine on the corner of the bed and completely untuck and loosen the sheets and covers to allow the tube to move freely. It's on 24-7, so he was also umbilical corded to the outlet. Steve struggled to get comfortable and got highly annoyed at everything. I can only imagine that being home he just wanted everything to be back to normal, but it just wasn't.

We were told that he would have the wound vac for about three weeks. During those first three weeks, a wound care specialist from home care services came in to change the dressing on the wound vac and check on the healing progress. Although grateful to have had an expert, this guy was on the creepy side. We didn't feel like he was the most sanitary, he had pet hair all over his clothes, and his mannerisms and conversation were off-putting. On top of Steve's anticipation to get the wound vac removed, not having a home care professional that made him feel at ease made time stand still. We tried to have him come late afternoon, so that I would be home from work to help be a buffer. One day I finally asked him if he could teach me how to change out the dressing. I figured if he taught me how to do it, he wouldn't have to come any more. He was happy to impart his knowledge, and I successfully changed out Steve's wound dressings a couple times and that was the end to home care services.

Meanwhile, during that time frame Steve's health insurance had contacted him to let him know that his short-term disability was about to run out. He had to go through the process of paperwork and phone interviews in order to get things extended. A ginormous thank you to the lady in human resources at Sports Authority who kept Steve's situation in mind. Her foresight and thinking of the big picture way back in September, when this drama all started and as the company was going out of business, had allowed Steve to be set up with short-term disability to begin with.

The bigger blessing to me learning how to take care of Steve's wound care needs was that as the three-week marker approached, his healing was nowhere near complete, so at least I could take care of him. Sadly, the new year was approaching and that created a new set of challenges on the health insurance front. Sports Authority had filed bankruptcy in March of 2016 and slowly started closing stores through the end of August. Although we knew he would be facing a new job at some point, Steve's job was one of the most secure and there were still quite a few people working out of the corporate offices when Steve was admitted to the hospital for the first time. A lot had happened, both for Steve and on the bankruptcy front, and he was officially going to lose his job on December 30, 2016, and in-turn lose his insurance as of December 31, 2016.

Thankfully, the VA coverage I had applied for on Steve's behalf back in October, had been accepted. On December 29, Steve and I spent the day at the VA; getting a wheelchair, seeing the wound care specialists, a primary care physician, and made sure he was set up for future appointments and connected into their system.

It was hard to lose the civilian insurance because that meant he would no longer be able to see the doctors and staff that had been treating him up to this point - the ones who knew the details of his situation and had seen him through the six surgeries. He basically had to start all over with lining up all the doctors and specialists.

His first stop was an appointment with a primary care doctor, then he was passed along to the vascular department, hematology department, and wound care specialists. He had to recount everything that had happened to him up to this point. Although it was over a short period of time, so much had happened, and he was drugged for so much of it that he had very little details to share. That meant I tried to take him to the majority of his appointments so I could recap and give the necessary details so he could receive proper care.

Steve was using me for his at-home wound care, but now that he was being treated by the VA, the wound care specialists there were having him come in three times a week. Although I tried to attend all of Steve's appointments, if nothing else than because of his memory issues, there was no way I could make three appointments a week.

After one of the visits I didn't attend, I got a phone call from one of the ladies with the wound care team. She said they wanted to know what exactly I was using because they were surprised at how rapidly he was healing in between visits. Steve had told them that I was using essential oils but couldn't say for sure what all I was doing or using. I was a little timid to share, however, when she told me to keep it up, I felt more comfortable sharing. My essential oil journey was still new to me. My thoughts were to use Melaleuca (Tea Tree) to help keep infections at bay, Frankincense for healthy inflammation and cellular repair, and Helichrysum, as needed, for bleeding issues.

His wound care specialist team at the VA were some of sweetest and most patient ladies I've ever met. They knew I was willing and wanting to help, so invited me to join Steve at his next appointment and watch me change out his dressing and see my technique. They taught me their tips and tricks so I could once again take over the wound dressing changes, and Steve would be able to taper down his visits to once a week and so on. I can't tell you how much that meant to Steve. It was mentally wearing on him. Initially to have someone come to our home three days a week to care for him and now he was having to drive three days a week. The ladies remained impressed with how quickly Steve was healing in-between his visits with them. What felt like an eternity to Steve (and I) apparently was totally normal and, in Steve's case, better than expected given the situation with the Prednisone.

Steve's mental fortitude continued to impress me and everyone around us. On February 4, 2017, we were presented with an opportunity to go to a Colorado Mammoth Lacrosse game at the Pepsi Center. Steve decided to bring his forearm crutches but use a wheelchair to get in and out of the event center. While we were there, we were fortunate enough to be in a suite with a private bathroom, which made the experience pleasurable with little to no issues, especially given that Steve was having to carry the wound vac around. On March 29, we went to the Denver Art Museum for the Star Wars and the Power of Costume exhibit. Again, Steve opted for the wheelchair, but we brought along the crutches so he could get closer and be able to use the restroom easier.

Our anniversary is on April 1, and we continued our tradition of going to The Melting Pot. It's an old building that has rich history. In the early 1900's it was a library, and in 1965 it was converted into a police department and then a jail until 1977. The interior is unique with multiple levels, small, steep staircases and lots of nooks and crannies. If you've ever been, you know it takes a few hours to complete a meal, so that typically means having to go to the bathroom at least once. Steve courageously handled our visit and navigated through the unique interior with no issues.

 Danette Penrod is 🥰 feeling loved.
April 1, 2017 · 👥   ···

Happy 15th Anniversary my love!

Graduating to a Prosthetic

From December 2016 to March 2017 was much of the same routine. The work-life-mom-caregiver balancing act. I was changing out Steve's dressing a minimum of once per day. Depending on the activities and how the wound was feeling, sometimes it was more. While he was healing from the physical wound, he was also learning to cope with the mental anguish of everything going on. Constantly being attached to a machine, not being able to do physical therapy or attempt walking, being jobless, and all the other mind games that came with this situation.

The wound vacuum that was supposed to take three weeks and be off before the end of January, finally came off on February 21, 2017. I'll never forget on my birthday, March 10, 2017, Steve was fitted with his first socket and stood on his own, unassisted by crutches, for the first time since the amputation. Unfortunately, I saw it via text, but I sat there in my office with the biggest grin and tears of joy streaming down my face. I was so proud and overwhelmed by the hope of "normalcy" that it meant.

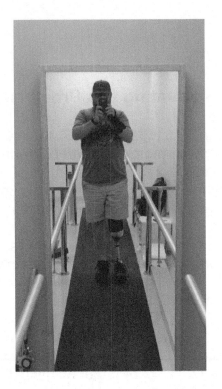

As Steve became mobile his weight started shifting, and he filtered through nine different sockets. This led to new amputee life challenges. His residual limb developed horrible sores. Steve said they burn like crazy, as if someone is holding a match to your skin. They don't look pretty either. They start off similar to an under the skin blemish, just a raised, red bump. But then it surfaces, bursts open, and creates an open sore.

I distinctly remember coming home from work one day to find a tube of Vagisil sitting on the nightstand (yes, the feminine hygiene product). I asked Steve why in the world he had it. He shared that his prosthetist had recommended it to help with the burning sensation his sores created. In fact, he said "I don't know what you ladies have going on down

there, but Brad said that it should help take the burn away."
Hum, okay. I walked over and grabbed the tube, flipped it
over and read the ingredients – basically water, mineral oil,
aloe and a bunch of words I can't pronounce. I asked him if
he might want to try something more natural and he was
totally up for experimenting.

My natural solutions mind-set went to clove oil as a numbing
agent for the burning, and an all-natural multi-purpose
ointment that contains great skin soothing essential oils.
Although it was my hope, to my surprise, within seconds of
putting a dab of clove oil on one of the sores, Steve said the
burning pain had subsided. The natural ointment not only
ended up helping to heal the sores quickly but left no traces
of scarring or discoloration on the skin.

When we saw the results of those two solutions, it got my
wheels spinning. I wanted to create something that we could
apply proactively, to hopefully help prevent the sores from
fully developing. After a little research, I created a residual
limb serum. A concoction of Lavender, Tea Tree, and
Copaiba essential oils in a base of carrier oil.

It worked too! It became part of our bedtime routine. Every
night as Steve took his leg off for the day, as we were getting
into bed, I would treat his residual limb by massaging my
essential oil concoction all over and would spot treat any
areas that needed some extra TLC with the natural ointment.
Although we did learn when I would go out of town, or
especially when our schedules shifted and I would go to bed
before him, that you have to be diligent with applying the
serum.

Steve was blessed that our fight to get him pain-free prior to
the amputation worked to minimize the phantom pain

situation. Although they happened pretty frequently, Steve's descriptions were more like sensations or irritations, not really pain. He said sometimes it would feel like his foot had been asleep and had that tingling feeling. He would also get random jolts that would send a quick zinger all the way down his leg into his foot. In the beginning we tried to determine if anything in particular caused them, something he'd eaten, a topic of conversation, or weather. Unfortunately, we never did find a correlation to when he had phantom sensations.

I was always on the hunt for another natural solution to help dissipate the phantom sensations altogether, and I found it by accident. I'd found an essential oil and botanical supplement that was formulated to calm the mind, encouraging the user to adapt to stressful situations and acclimate to new surroundings. With all the mental fatigue and changes Steve had been under, I thought it might help him with his mental state. As it turned out, not only did it help with his overall mental wellness, but the supplement also contains 100mg of naturally sourced GABA. GABA is a quieting neurotransmitter that is sometimes known as the "breaks of the brain," because it lowers the activity of neural cells in the brain and central nervous system. All that to say, it worked to spread out the phantom sensations, Steve can go weeks at a time now with none of those strange feelings.

The Aftermath

There are lots of things that change after someone loses part of their leg, starting with the most obvious, you can't just get up and walk. We were told by another amputee that at some point, in the beginning most likely, that Steve will forget about his leg being gone. The example we were given was getting up to go to the bathroom in the middle of the night. As of this book release (October, 2022) we're six years into the journey and it's not happened yet. Steve says that it will never happen, that there's hardly a moment that goes by that he's not reminded, in some form or fashion, that he's missing part of his leg.

Thankfully as of now Steve's mobility is only limited in two places – the bedroom and bathroom. Other than creating space to add in a wound care station and places to set or store extra body parts, our bedroom wasn't altered. The bathroom is another story. For the record we had talked about remodeling it for years but hadn't gotten around to it yet, and now I know why. You can't wear a prosthetic in the shower and that creates mobility issues. When you add soap and water into the mix, you've got a recipe for potential trouble.

We had beautiful brass framed sliding glass doors on a cream-colored tub. The handful of pink flowers that adorned the once white tiles added a pop of color to accent the baby blue flowers on the worn linoleum floor. I mean it was a shame to get rid of the rich history and dirt that had grown in there over the years. Hahaha!

In all seriousness, we wanted to do something more aesthetic and functional than simply adding a grab bar and a bench. In order to make the bathroom bigger we removed the closet in the master bedroom that was only being used to house a television and a few winter coats as well as the linen closet in the hallway. We took the shower/tub combo out and created a walk-in shower that was wide and long enough to accompany a bench and not require a door. We added cabinets in the interior of the bathroom to replace the linen closet that used to be in the hallway, making it easier to access towels, toilet paper and all other needed bathroom backstock products. The design has worked well for our family's needs, and we have no regrets with the changes.

Steve puts his prosthetic on in the morning when he wakes up and rarely takes it off until he showers or goes to bed. We've learned this is pretty unusual in comparison to how long other amputees wear their prosthetic. Steve's philosophy is he wants to maintain as normal of mobility as possible for the entirety of the day. This has created some challenges for his residual limb and the wear and tear it adds to all the components that go into the prosthetic. On the flip side, it means not having to remodel any other parts of our house to make it accessible.

Blood Thinners

When Steve was leaving the hospital, he was on three different anticoagulants; Aspirin, Warfarin, plus he had to give himself shots of Enoxaparin for ten days. It seemed like it was a lot and I was a bit concerned, but obviously trusted the hematology team to be doing what they felt was in Steve's best interest given what they knew about the situation. It was explained to me that the ten days of shots was for the acute situation and to prevent him from having to come back to the hospital for additional clotting. I was still confused by their thoughts around his clotting, since he was never deemed to have had an infection, and the clotting was understandable and explainable when you consider them sending him home with holes dripping blood and me using a natural coagulant with the Helichrysum.

I also knew that Warfarin is a controlled drug that required regular visits to the hospital to have his blood drawn to monitor his INR closely, so I saw the potential problem that would cause a number of appointments, especially in the beginning as they figured out the appropriate dosing. So, I asked them how long they anticipated him being on the drug. The answer was not definitive, but six months to a year was likely, with a potential for life, if the Minimal Change Disease didn't get reversed.

Steve was officially cleared of MCD in March of 2017 and was taken off Prednisone. However, he remained on Warfarin for months...and then years. While Warfarin is considered a safe drug to take for long periods of time, I had growing concerns about Steve staying on a drug that wasn't necessary.

The drug came with a medical bracelet, to identify the drug to first responders, due to potential internal bleeding issues, however, Steve didn't wear it. It's also a drug that has interactions and there's an increased risk of bleeding with kidney problems, proneness to falling, and alcohol. Well, though not a current issue anymore, he'd certainly had kidney problems and without answers as to how he developed MCD or if it would come back, I wasn't sure how this factored into the health of his kidneys. And not to rub salt in the wound, he'd already fallen a few times prior to getting the prosthetic and could absolutely have a higher-than-normal chance of falling. The doctors said having a beer here and there is okay when you're on Warfarin, but I felt Steve pushed the limits without even considering the consequences.

After years of Steve being on this drug complaining about having to get his INR checked regularly, which was once a month at this point, and not taking the proper precautions for someone on a blood thinner, my constant questioning him about it ultimately led to a fight. My perspective was that he hadn't needed to be on the drug since March of 2017, but at most through the end of that year. The problem, in my opinion, was that he'd switched providers. He'd started at a civilian hospital and was currently being treated by the VA. I don't think they'd done the research to know or understand that this wasn't necessarily a lifelong drug.

When I questioned Steve about it from his perspective the drug was saving his life, and he was under the impression that he had a propensity for blood clots. Here I was insisting that he talk to his providers about it and all he was hearing was that I clearly didn't care about his life. I was mortified at this realization and told him that if he legit thought it was saving his life then, yes, he should stay on it, and I'd never bring it up again. However, I also thought that he needed to live like a person who is on the drug and that he should stop complaining about having to go to the VA to have his INR checked.

As an aside, going to the VA was mentally taxing. You don't schedule appointments for blood work. You show up, grab a number and wait to be called. In the meantime, you're exposed to a plethora of personality types, varying levels of mental capacities, sicknesses, and disabilities, not to mention the reminder that he was there because of an issue that he had to live with for the rest of his life.

I never did bring up Warfarin again, but he did. Many times! Remember the short-term memory issue? Sometimes he'd go a couple weeks until he had an INR check-up to mention it, other times we'd talk about it five times in one week. Eventually, as in five years later, now into 2020, we were able to have another heart-to-heart about it. I explained what the civilian hematology doctors' plans were for why he was on Warfarin and how long he needed to be on it. We agreed that we knew the early warning signs to be on the lookout for with MCD, so there was really no need to continue taking a drug that technically wasn't doing anything for him, other than the side effects. Like frequent nose bleeds and unexplained bruising. He also had this weird skin condition on his "good" leg, specifically on his calf and foot. He had all these tiny red dots, like every pore was infected. On his foot they pooled together and it was a deep purple color. Within a couple weeks of going off the Warfarin that condition cleared and he hasn't had any issues since.

Drama with the Mama

Prior to Steve's amputation he would have weekly conversations with his parents. His mom and I had a good relationship and texted regularly, if nothing else than to share pictures and happenings in our son's world. After their visit with us, and Steve had gone back to the hospital just four days after his release from the amputation surgery, the communication with them started to get sporadic.

My thought was that it was in relation to Steve and his dad's fight. I was unclear why the communication with me had started getting rocky. I was still sending updates and pictures, but they came with little or no reply other than talk about our Christmas wish lists. As we were walking Steve into pre-op for his washout surgery on December 2, I got a text from my mother-in-law asking why I wasn't telling them anything. The first thought that came to mind was confusion. I had been updating them. I'd sent the same text to her as I had the rest of the family to let them know that Steve was being admitted back to the hospital and having another surgery. The second thought was that this situation, like the rest of his journey had been, was very sudden. I'd literally just gotten to the hospital when they were taking him into pre-op. The next morning, I got a text asking if I could let her know why everyone was pissed off at them. My response turned the tables and asked why they thought anyone was mad at them and that it felt the opposite, that they were upset with us. Her response was "No of course not."

The text conversation that ensued:
Date: Saturday, December 3, 2016 at 11:05 AM
When dad made his comment to Steve "It's time for you to grow up & be a man" that was hard to hear. Then for dad to get angry & spend the rest of the evening downstairs was immature. Steve took the high road & has not been dwelling on how that made him feel. And there hasn't been an apology. On top of which, you guys have not reached out to him/us hardly at all since your visit. That's why it feels like your upset with us. Why do you feel we're upset with you?

> **Date: Saturday, December 3, 2016 at 7:25 PM**
> I am sorry for that situation. I know Jon says things but I know he really doesn't mean it. We no longer feel like we are welcome from Scott and Kara. It so hard to hear what he said and feels. Scott never talked to his dad at all when we were there. Sunday was very hard knowing Steve hurt so bad but you heard Kara she couldn't even introduce me to her friend. She belongs to him?? I can't believe she said that. So we just don't call at all and I am sorry that we hurt you in the process.

Date: Saturday, December 3, 2016 at 7:32 PM
I'm confused why the situation with Scott/Kara has anything to do with us. I honestly must have missed the whole introduction ordeal, that doesn't seem like Kara, but I'm sorry if that happened.

Date: Saturday, December 3, 2016 at 7:38 PM
Steve said he thinks it was in reference to Casey's wife...when she walked in, Kara said to you & "she belongs to him (Casey)".

Date: Saturday, December 3, 2016 at 7:42 PM
I didn't think so.

Date: Saturday, December 3, 2016 at 7:43 PM
I think you're trying to hard to make things difficult. Scott was told to have a nice f'ing life & then yet made the choice to pick you up & hang out at our house, invited us over there, etc. I just think emotions are running high & feelings were hurt. I know Scott wants a good relationship with you guys. And I don't want OUR relationship to get messed up in the meantime.

Date: Saturday, December 3, 2016 at 8:03 PM
We have different opinions and don't think they do but won't let it interfere with us...

Date: Saturday, December 3, 2016 at 8:06 PM
That makes me sad, but we'll agree to disagree on them & just focus on us. ♥

My frustration grew the next day when we had a phone conversation. It was all about Steve's brother Scott and how hurt she was that Scott had shared his feelings about her back in June. To this day, I don't understand why what happened with one child has any bearing about how you handle the other relationship, especially when their son almost lost his life and was experiencing life as a new amputee.

Our texts between January and March seemed fairly normal; gifts for Talon's birthday, sending pictures, discussing health insurance, and updates about Steve. I sent texts with pictures on April 8, 11, 13, 14, 15, and 16 that yielded no responses. On the 17th I flat out asked if she was still interested in what's going on in our life. The response came back on the 18ᵗʰ with no real reason why she hadn't replied to anything in ten days. Instead, she wanted to know why Steve hadn't returned her text.

That text was in regard to Steve's sister, Stacey's donation, if they were speaking, and if he was speaking to his birth mother [Note: more info about the donation will be included in The Sister chapter]. Steve had responded to her, that yes, he was speaking to his sister and no he was not speaking to his birth mother. Though he was asked whether his brother Scott was also speaking to their sister, Steve didn't respond with an answer. He instead texted back asking her a series of questions which went unanswered.

Date: Friday, April 28, 2017 at 8:46 AM
It's almost been 2 weeks since our last text. We are trying to be open & honest with you guys, but how can we move forward & have a relationship if you're unwilling to communicate? What can we do to prove our love & desire to have you in our lives? Will you please let us know what we did/didn't do that's upset or hurt you guys? We're ALL suffering. Please help us to get this situation resolved.

Date: Saturday, April 29, 2017 at 9:04 PM
We just thought there should be some down time. So many hurtful things have been said on both sides or not been said. I am just hoping that there hasn't been to much said or done. So we are doing some soul searching....

Date: Saturday, April 29, 2017 at 9:06 PM
What have Steve and/or I said (or not) that has been hurtful?
What can we do to put this behind us?

She never responded to my questions and that was the last text I got from her. In fact, that was that last communication any of us had with Steve's parents for nearly three months. Then she started asking me for pictures of Talon to which I responded, "Would you be open to a phone call?" She thought I meant talking to Talon and tried to set something up with him, but my reply was, "I meant a phone call with me." When that was **not** responded to by the next morning, I texted back:

Date: Saturday, July 22, 2017 at 10:19 AM
You cannot be grandparents until you're loving parents & have a relationship with your kids. We want to move forward, but the more time that goes by allows the boys to callous themselves from the pain you're causing. They've already had their birth mom "abandon" them, why are you doing the same? We're all hurting, but we can't make amends if there's not open communication on all sides.

I received no response and in September we received a package in the mail that had a lot of Steve's childhood memorabilia – baby books, pictures, trophies, and the like. I sent her a text to thank her and let them know that Steve had appreciated getting his childhood stuff. I asked if they were moving but got no reply and no further communication until November.

Date: Thursday, November 2, 2017 at 5:43 PM
The shirt for Talon is awesome! Thank you for thinking of him. I dreamed about you guys last night. You've been weighing heavy on my heart. I'm truly having a very hard time with our lack of relationship.

> **Date: Thursday, November 2, 2017 at 5:55 PM**
> There hasn't been a day we haven't thought or talked about all of you.

Date: Thursday, November 2, 2017 at 6:20 PM
Sorry, was cooking. Then why aren't we talking? Did we do something?

> **Date: Friday, November 3, 2017 at 12:41 PM**
> Will talk soon. Can I have Scott and Steve's, yours and Kara's email. Just updating my phone.

And once again silence. There was some back-n-forth about Christmas presents being delivered and a Merry Christmas along with a thank you for sending pictures Christmas morning, but other than that, no communication with me until July, 2018.

> **Date: Friday, July 13, 2018 at 11:44 AM**
> Hello....We just want to apologize to you also and hope you can forgive us... we really felt Scott was very upset with us so we also thought Steve was to. One little thing just grows and grows. We do love u guys very much...

Date: Sunday, July 16, 2018 at 8:19 PM
I love and miss u very much and of course Steve and
Talon.

Date: Thursday, July 19, 2018 at 2:58 PM
How bad have I hurt our relationship?

I chose not to respond via text. I contemplated about how I
felt and how long their lack of communication had been
going on. I was certainly beyond hurt, but at the end of the
day all I wanted was for everyone to get along. I conceded to
reach out and called her that weekend. We had a decent,
albeit awkward, conversation.

Date: Thursday, July 26, 2018 at 2:49 PM
Is there anything else that we can do so u guys aren't
mad? I know Steve is....

Date: Thursday, July 26, 2018 at 2:53 PM
I don't think mad is the right word. I think he's weirded out by
the whole situation. It was a long time of not communicating,
so please just be patient, persistent & loving.

Date: Friday, August 3, 2018 at 1:37 PM
I'm always thinking of u guys. Hoping u and Steve r
being able to forgive us.

Date: Friday, August 3, 2018 at 1:41 PM
Forgiveness is easy for me. Though I may not understand
what happened and was truly hurt, I'm able to see past that
and focus on a positive future. You will run into a harder time
with Steve, as you can tell. It's not that he can't or hasn't

forgiven, it's his lack of understanding. I think he wants/needs answers.

Date: Friday, August 3, 2018 at 1:48 PM
I know. It started with the fight they had. Jon didn't mean the way he said what he did. Just a lot of misunderstandings. It ended up being a mole hill into a mountain. I known I should of fought harder but they had to work it out. Then I couldn't take it anymore. We had a lot of talks. It was really stupid.

Date: Friday, August 3, 2018 at 1:51 PM
Stubborn Penrod genes!

Date: Thursday, August 9, 2018 at 8:09 AM
Hi..just wanted to stay in touch and say that I miss you guys. Looked like u and Talon had a great time at the water park.

Date: Thursday, August 9, 2018 at 8:15 AM
Hi, good morning. It was a blast! Then he went camping & didn't get home until after 6 last night. He's around today.

Date: Thursday, August 9, 2018 at 8:25 AM
Will call when Jon gets home. Can we talk a little each day or so? Have missed talking to you...... I know everyone thinks we r horrible but am trying to repair everything.

Date: Thursday, August 9, 2018 at 8:28 AM
Yes, of course. Don't put that projection out there. That's not my stance at all. Just be patient, diligent & loving with the boys.

> **Date: Thursday, August 9, 2018 at 8:32 AM**
> We will.. Scott and dad and I had a long talk the other night. Think it helped alot. Will with Steve. Have talked to Stacey every sunday.

Date: Thursday, August 9, 2018 at 8:32 AM
That's great!

Somewhere along the way, Steve's dad had been diagnosed with COPD. That wasn't a huge surprise as he'd been a long-time smoker and though fortunate enough not to have suffered a heart attack, he did have a quadruple bypass back in 2015. With the holistic health journey, I'd been on since right before Steve's medical drama started, I had shared with Carla some things that I thought might help Jon. Along with those conversations about natural solutions to help him came questions for her. On Sunday, the 11th, I texted her some pictures of Talon from a church event we'd gone to, along with a success story from a couple I'd met there, who were able to get off an over-the-counter drug by replacing it with one of the products I'd shared with her.

> **Date: Thursday, August 16, 2018 at 6:29 PM**
> Hi, how r you? Has ur week been going okay? Talked to Talon today. Not looking forward to school. Dad is going to talk to Stacey on Monday. Good news. Do u talk to her very often?

Date: Thursday, August 16, 2018 at 7:48 PM
Doing good. Just took Talon to a sushi dinner for our last summer meal. Week has been long, but decent. Stacey & I used to talk at least once a week, but the last couple months have been more scarce as I don't have as much free time. I thought they were having lunch tomorrow?

> **Date: Thursday, August 16, 2018 at 7:53 PM**
> They were but had something come up for tomorrow so Monday. I can't believe he likes sushi. He was fun to talk to today.

> **Date: Saturday, August 18, 2018 at 10:29 AM**
> Are u still mad at me? I just hope we can have a good relationship.

Date: Saturday, August 18, 2018 at 10:38 AM
What!?! No. I was never mad. Hurt by the lack of understanding of why you wouldn't talk to me. I'm ready to move on.

Carla had purchased some natural solution products from me earlier in the month, so we'd had communications around usage tips and me checking in with her. When I reached out, her responses always seemed to be embedded with a random thought or question about someone being mad, not getting a response from Steve, or questions about communications or visits with Stacey.

I always encouraged both of Steve's parents to be consistent with their communications and patient with the responses or lack thereof. I tried to gently remind them that they made the decision to not speak to us without reason for basically a year and a half during the hardest time in our lives to date.

Jon's health weighed on me when I'd hear that things weren't going that well. In October, 2018, his COPD had gotten so bad that he was put on oxygen, which seemed to help him a lot, though I can't say it helped my mind from racing. I felt an enormous amount of pressure to try to get this parent-sibling relationship mended quickly for fear that it would be too late.

> **Date: Tuesday, November 13, 2018 at 12:23 PM**
> I'm sorry I haven't texted or called but I am not sure if u want me to or how you feel about me. I would like to mend our relationship. But if you don't I will try to understand. I love you. I know you are busy also.

Date: Tuesday, November 13, 2018 at 2:15 PM
I'm sorry that you don't feel like you know how I feel. I've always wanted and tried to maintain a relationship with you. I was hurt when you needed space, but we can't change that. I'm anxious to move forward.

My apologies too, I've had you on my mind, as a matter of fact I started a text to you last night until I realized that it was after 11 your time.

> **Date: Thursday, November 29, 2018 at 12:43 PM**
> Steve is still upset with us?? Why he won't talk to us…

Date: Thursday, November 29, 2018 at 4:48 PM
Sorry, had a full day. I just asked him, he said he'd call this
weekend.

> **Date: Friday, December 14, 2018 at 3:06 PM**
> I see Steve hasn't forgiven us.

Date: Friday, December 14, 2018 at 3:08 PM
I not very happy with him for telling you he'd call last
weekend and then not follow through. I think he needs more
answers/closure. He's really struggling with not
understanding what HE did.

> **Date: Friday, December 14, 2018 at 3:11 PM**
> Did u see what I texted him? Danette I really can't say
> he did anything. Just Thinking everyone didn't care.

Date: Friday, December 14, 2018 at 3:15 PM
Yes, I saw the text. Made it sound like he got lumped into the
drama with Scott. He also knows how frequently I tried to
communicate with you until you asked me to stop, so saying
you didn't think we cared doesn't make sense. I'm just telling
you what I know, I understand it can't be changed. Please
continue to be patient, loving and persistent.

> **Date: Friday, December 14, 2018 at 3:26 PM**
> I know Jon said hurtful things but didn't mean it to be
> and then they got into it, jon got mad and thought also
> he didn't care. It is just a horrible mess. Wish we
> could take it all back. Just tell him he didn't and things
> got taken all wrong. We do love you guys very much.

Date: Friday, December 14, 2018 at 3:33 PM
I think the timing with the amputation doesn't help. He feels abandoned (my word not his) at a time when he was going through a huge struggle and needed love & support, not negativity or drama. His life has forever changed. I'm not sure what to do to right the past, Steve has to want to forgive and move forward. I'm working on him, but as you know it's slow moving.

> **Date: Friday, December 14, 2018 at 3:36 PM**
> I know and I appreciate it very much., We will keep trying and praying.

Date: Friday, December 14, 2018 at 3:36 PM
Me too.

> **Date: Sunday, January 13 2019 at 9:51 AM**
> Good Morning, hope u guys are doing good. Have a question, are we not trying hard enough to have Steve come back and talk to us?? I know how the feeling is!!!!!

Date: Sunday, January 13 2019 at 9:57 AM
Good morning. I'm not sure what to say or do anymore. Steve's not being very responsive to me about the situation. About the only thing I can say is he doesn't understand why his dad hasn't tried to maintain a relationship, basically since the amputation. I'm not giving up!

> **Date: Sunday, January 13 2019 at 10:12 AM**
> Like father like son. They don't show much emotion or caring sometimes. Even though they do care very much. They don't know how to show it. Is Steve home, I will have Jon try calling him.

Date: Sunday, January 13 2019 at 10:14 AM
No, he's in San Diego. His buddy's retirement from the Navy.

Communication tapered back off again to surface level stuff about birthday/holiday presents and support in using the natural solutions, especially since I'd given them a bunch of stuff to help with Jon's respiratory health issues for Christmas.

We'd recently planned to take a trip back to Illinois in June to be able to help Demi (Steve's sister Stacey's daughter) celebrate her graduation from college. We hadn't seen Steve's parents since October, 2016 and we were going to be 20 minutes from their home so, of course, whether to see them or not was part of our conversations.

Date: Wednesday, March 27, 2019 at 6:10 AM
I talked briefly to Steve last night about going back there, which naturally brought you guys up. What I can tell you is this, which he has said to me numerous times before. He just doesn't understand why his dad doesn't make any effort to communicate with him.

From Steve's perspective (in a nutshell), after his amputation Jon hurt him, we started talking to Stacey, you guys stopped talking to us. He doesn't understand. The apology he got was I'm sorry, I was just joking. If that were true then it's really confusing why y'all stopped all communication with us.

I think you just have to be honest. And keep trying.

> **Date: Wednesday, March 27, 2019 at 11:21 AM**
> I will talk to Jon again..........

Date: Sunday, April 21, 2019 at 11:06 AM
Happy Easter! Thank you for Talon's generous gift. Also, we bought our tickets to come out there. Would you guys be willing to meet with all the kids, maybe May 31st? Not sure the next time they'll all be together in IL.

> **Date: Sunday, April 21, 2019 at 11:06 AM**
> Happy Easter!!!!!! Of course. That means Steve, Scott, Stacey don't want to see us?

Date: Sunday, April 21, 2019 at 11:07 AM
What!?! I don't understand the question. I'm making sure you guys are open to seeing Stacey, Steve & Scott.

> **Date: Sunday, April 21, 2019 at 11:07 AM**
> Okay….yes of course.

As our vacation got closer and closer there was still no outreach from Jon or Carla to any of the kids. There was also no mention of it in what little communication we had either. Friday, May 31 rolled around and I texted Carla to see when we could come over. The siblings had collectively decided that they wouldn't be joining Talon and I when we visited Jon and Carla since they didn't feel there was any effort on their parent's part to mend any of their relationships.

Talon and I had a short, okay visit. Carla took Talon outside so I could have a heart-to-heart with Jon. I simply shared Steve's perspective and thought that the ball was in his court. He asked me why he would want to have a relationship with someone that clearly didn't want a relationship with him and didn't love him. I almost laughed out loud. Oh, how the Penrod's think the same, I thought to myself. I shared that Steve had almost verbatim said those same words to me. I then reminded him that it was his choice not to speak to his son for a year and a half and he still hadn't given an explanation. I left him with the fact that the ball was in his court. He needed to act like a loving, caring father and make amends with his children.

Sadly, nothing changed. In fact, things resorted back to the communications with me being very minimal again too. Carla would simply respond to my texts with updates and pictures of Talon. Steve and his dad had tried to have a couple of phone conversations, but nothing changed.

Date: Monday, October 28, 2019 at 3:52 PM
Hey. Wanted to check-in with you guys. You've been very quiet.

Date: Tuesday, November 5, 2019 at 5:38 AM
So, you guys aren't speaking to us again? I'm so confused. The last conversation Steve had with Jon was pretty decent (and normal) and JON said he was going to call Steve back in a few days. So now he's doing to Steve what he was mad at Steve for doing to him (saying he was going to call, but then not)?

> **Date: Tuesday, November 5, 2019 at 8:28 AM**
> We are confused also. When Steve said he would talk to me when he is ready, we both took it as he didn't want to talk. I asked what I did and never got an answer. I am guessing I am the problem. They are all upset and do not like me. When he said that that upset Jon.

Date: Sunday, November 10, 2019 at 1:34 PM
I'm going to be extremely blunt.

This tit-for-tat crap has to stop.

Facts: Steve did not do anything to warrant you guys not speaking to him for over a year. He needed your love and support & instead was met with silence. I've told you before that consistency and patience is what it's going to take. How can you expect him to just forget and move on, when that's not the example he's being given. Jon said that he didn't feel like Steve wanted to speak to him or loved him and that's EXACTLY what Steve tells me about you guys.

Don't forget YOU guys made the choice not to speak to US, so to put it in Steve's court doesn't make sense to me.

> **Date: Sunday, November 10, 2019 at 9:51 PM**
> I have one question to ask and it is just for me. They don't want to talk or have anything to do with me do they?? I have to know for me...

Date: Sunday, November 10, 2019 at 9:54 PM
I can only sorta speak for Steve. It's my understanding that from his perspective his dad has chosen to disassociate himself from him and he feels like you're the one in control of that (I think). Honestly I'm not entirely sure anymore, just that he's been extremely hurt and the only way he knows how to handle it is to pretend he's fine.

> **Date: Monday, November 11, 2019 at 7:16 AM**
> Knowing how his dad is I can't believe they would think i would have any control of how he feels. But believe me I try.

Date: Monday, November 11, 2019 at 7:18 AM
Not that you have control over Jon, but it being your choice to stop talking to all of us due to hurt feelings (warranted) and then the perceptions you placed on us. By you choosing not to speak to us "controls" Jon not speaking to us.

> **Date: Monday, November 11, 2019 at 7:22 AM**
> It was not all me. But if they want to blame me......

Date: Monday, November 11, 2019 at 7:34 AM
This isn't about blame, it's about choice. Be it you, Jon or both of you, neither of you spoke to Steve, Talon or I despite all my efforts. I appreciate that you had a change of heart and want us back in your life (or did), but the stubborn Penrod blood runs deep. It's, in my opinion, it's up to Jon to show compassion & grace towards his children for whatever wrongs he feels they've done to him. He, as their father, needs to be the example of what he wants from them.

I feel this situation has viciously snowballed out of control, and honestly not even sure how to repair. But IF you want a relationship with Steve, starting with telling him why you want him in your life and attempting regular communication might be good.

Once again, I was met with silence. The next text I received was December 2 – just a note to let me know about a Christmas package I should be receiving. Steve finally called Carla in mid-December and let her have an earful about why he was over her. I made sure to text her to let her know that although I respected and honored his feelings, they were his and not mine.

Date: Thursday, February 6, 2020 at 5:14 PM
I hope you're not lumping us into Scott's drama again. I've
never understood why you stopped talking to me? I've
always tried to maintain a relationship with you. Hope you're
both doing well. Thinking about ya.

Date: Thursday, February 25, 2020 at 6:52 AM
Talon said he hadn't heard from you in a while. Are you done
with him too?

Date: Saturday, March 21, 2020 at 9:28 PM
Thinking about you both. Hope you're doing well & healthy.
Talon is especially concerned about grandpa having COPD.
I assured him that y'all are staying home, but he said it's
really scary.

It broke my heart to not be responded to, but beyond how I
was feeling, I was concerned how Talon was feeling.
Wondering if he noticed, thought it was normal, or even
cared. In early December Carla finally reached out asking for
Christmas ideas for Talon, while making a comment that she
wasn't sure if I'd respond. I answered with the requested
ideas and a simple message that I wasn't the one who
stopped trying, or caring, or loving. The rest of the month
was silence other than Carla asking me for pictures of Talon,
which I chose not to send. By early January, 2021, Carla had
asked me for a phone conversation, which I agreed to have.
It wasn't the greatest for her, as I didn't hold back my
frustration and hurt over the lack of relationship. She got
vulnerable, sharing her feelings, hurt, and the pain in
assuming that everyone hated her.

Our communications picked up as fairly normal, but the underlying motivation was trying to get Steve to talk to them again. By this point Steve's dad, Jon, was getting worse with his COPD symptoms, so their motivation to try to make progress had shifted and had more of a sense of urgency. Talon also started receiving communications again, both calls and texts, which made my heart so happy.

On the other hand, Steve's heart was more than callused at this point. I did my best to breathe positivity into the situation, but our conversations about his parents were pretty few and far between. I honestly feel like that weighed on him too – the fact that he wasn't even thinking about them anymore. Or at least that's what he told me. I know it was a defense mechanism and I'll never understand how he felt.

By June, 2021 a little progress had been made, Steve had talked to his dad on the phone a few times. We were gearing up for a trip back to Illinois and this time Steve's brothers' family was going back at the same time. The siblings agreed to see their dad, and on July 15, 2021 the three siblings and their dad were together for the first time in over 35 years. It was also the first time they'd seen Steve, in person, since he was fitted with a prosthetic. There were a few questions about life as an amputee and the mechanics of his leg, but otherwise the short visit was superficial conversations about the weather, jobs, and what the kids were up to or into these days.

The time together was needed and I'm so glad it happened and that we have a photo to commemorate that special day. Funny though how a picture can give the appearance of one big happy family.

After our trip, communications between Carla and I got sporadic again. Mostly updates about Talon. On Monday, January 17, 2022, Jon died. At the time, Carla wasn't up for doing a memorial service, primarily since Jon didn't want anything. Neither of the boys had spoken very much with Carla since 2016 and they haven't spoken with her since his passing either. I had reached out by calling and texting but rarely got a text response – never a call or even an acknowledgement that I called. Since Jon was cremated, we decided to all go back to Illinois at the same time. In the summer of 2022, we had a ceremony for him. It was small and intimate with the military tribute being the best part.

The Sister

Right around the time of his amputation Steve's brother, Scott, and his wife, Kara, started a GoFundMe to help with our hospital bills and remodeling efforts. There were so many people whom I'd never met from Steve's former employer, Sports Authority, who donated. The outpouring from our friends and family and even Scott and Kara's friends and family was astounding to me.

A couple months after the amputation, I recall sitting in the sauna one morning and got a notification that we'd received another donation. I pulled it up and saw the generous amount. I was taken aback already and then saw the donation was from Steve's sister, Stacey. So many thoughts raced through my head. This gesture was not the act of the selfish person I'd been told about.

When I told Steve how much she donated, I think he was more shocked than I was. We chatted about it, and I told him that I felt the donation amount was a sacrifice. Then I asked him what he thought she'd have to gain from giving it. He almost sheepishly responded with "Nothing." I wanted to reach out to her, and Steve had given me permission, but ultimately, I decided that I didn't want to go down the path of getting to know my other sister-in-law if I would never have a relationship with her. So, I waited.

Perhaps it was the drugs, the amputation, the generous donation, or a combination of all of it, but Steve's heart was softened and he agreed to have a phone conversation with her on February 16, 2017. Over the next several months, Steve started to develop a relationship with his sister over the phone.

On May 19, 2017, Stacey and her 19-year-old daughter, Demi, flew out to Colorado to meet all of us and see her brothers for the first time in over 30 years. I reserved a private room at Hacienda Colorado, a great Mexican restaurant that already held weight in our family as a special place. It was a beautiful and intimate dinner for all of us as we learned about one another's favorite color, sports team, food preferences, and anything else we decided to share. Over their couple day trip, we enjoyed playing tourist and soaked up every bit of time together. It was perfect.

Since that trip we've developed a very close-knit relationship with Stacey, her husband Danny, and our niece, Demi. Stacey has been diligent about seeing us at last twice a year. The longest we went was during the pandemic and during that time there were a lot more phone calls and we even did family Zooms. It feels normal and natural to have them in our life, and with every conversation and in-person visit, the bond is solidified.

FAQs

Before we dive in, let me start this section off by expressing some gratitude.

I am beyond grateful that my husband is alive.

My gratitude extends out to our friends, family and acquaintances who supported us with prayers, visits, meals, cards, donations, flowers, gifts, and the most treasured of all, their time and energy to do all those things.

Did you file a lawsuit? This is by far the question we get asked the most. The short answer is we tried. The lawyer we signed with thought it was a slam dunk case and didn't do his due diligence. He didn't talk to Steve's surgeon until one and a half years post-surgery. We were butting up against the two-year statute of limitations for a medical malpractice when he called to tell us that he couldn't produce the expert witnesses we needed to win the case. Needless to say, we were extremely frustrated, but ultimately believe it's not what God had in store for us and have trusted that.

Does Steve drive? Yep! While he can and does sometimes drive with his left foot. Steve had hand controls installed in his truck. The hand controls allow him to not use either of his feet. You push a lever forward to go and you pull it back to stop. The steering wheel was fitted with a knob that allows him to make turns with only using one hand. There is a learning curve, and while you don't have to, he went through the proper channels to do driving lessons so that he'd be confident and comfortable using them.

How does Steve golf? Oddly enough Steve's golf game has gotten better since his amputation. My personal opinion is that it doesn't have anything to do with the prosthetic. He was able to play a lot of golf during the time he was healing. For about nine months, he was mobile but not able to work yet. So, sometimes he was able to golf three to four times a week. He had too many doctors' appointments to hold down a job, plus he was in limbo with not knowing what his capabilities or limitations were in trying to look for a new job, since Sports Authority had closed their doors for good right after the amputation.

Are family vacations different? The biggest difference in traveling is that we have to pay attention to accessible features. Walk-in showers are best, but if hotels only offer a tub-shower combo, then we have to find out if there's a bench or one we can rent. We also used to frequent water parks and that just hasn't been a thing since the amputation. Steve has gone swimming a few times, but doesn't have a water leg, so he sits on the edge and takes his leg off. The looks he gets are pretty priceless. At home Steve has forearm crutches that he'll use if he has to go to the bathroom in the middle of the night. When we're on vacation, he doesn't bring them and has been known to hop his way to the bathroom. I'm not a fan.

Does Steve consider himself disabled? The majority of the time Steve is as able-bodied as I am, in the way of mobility. Although he wears shorts all the time, if he didn't you wouldn't have any idea that he was an amputee. He does have a handicap placard, and yes, it gets used from time to time. I think it's important to have it for the rough days and for the days that haven't come our way yet – broken parts or other problems. Steve is also not sensitive to the words handicap or disabled. He chooses not to let the words, or condition, define him and makes jokes all the time.

My little Personal Service Announcement is that not everyone is as lighthearted about those terms. Know your audience, and if you don't, be cautious in how you use them – or just don't use them at all. The better term to use is accessible. The other thing is parking. If you don't have the legal right to park in an accessible parking spot, then don't...ever! Not even to just drop off something super quick and no one else is around.

Does Steve use a wheelchair? The short answer is no. While we are so grateful he has one in the event he needs it, thankfully he has not used his wheelchair since March of 2016. Plus, our home isn't able to fit a wheelchair. Because Steve wears his prosthetic from the moment he wakes up to the moment he goes to bed, he can have more wear and tear on the components that make up his prosthetic. And should there ever come a time when Steve isn't able to wear a prosthetic for a longer period of time, because he's waiting on parts or has a wound that has to heal, then he would likely use his forearm crutches. He also has a device called an iWALK, it's basically a hands-free crutch. It's not designed for amputees specifically, but it totally works for Steve's situation.

Did Steve suffer depression? The period of time after the amputation when Steve had the wound vac and was not super mobile was difficult. While I was gone at work was the worst. Steve was alone with his thoughts - struggling with mentally understanding why he was in this position, bored, hurting, uncomfortable, worried about not working, you name it. My return from work was certainly a highlight of his day, and he confided in me that although he would never act on it, thoughts of suicide did surface for him more than once. Not planning it out, but rather thoughts around why the blood clot didn't just kill him.

What does Steve say when people ask what happened?
He does have a couple go-to answers, depending on his mood and audience. "Bad things happen to good people," is the one reserved for strangers and sometimes kids, especially if he doesn't feel like chatting. I will say there are a lot of assumptions about Steve having lost his leg in combat. While he proudly served in the Navy, his response here is that no one shot it off. Steve has the utmost patience and compassion for the innocence of a child staring or asking what happened. However, there are some adults that are just plain rude and inappropriate. Steve has no problem putting them in their place either.

What has been the biggest challenge? Steve's answer is that an amputation isn't something you ever fully heal from. He's constantly reminded that his missing part of his leg and everyday there are irritations, both physically and mentally.

My answer is that we never got a reason why Steve got Minimal Change Disease. That coupled with seeing things in hindsight and thinking through the what if's – I would've advocated more in certain areas. For example, the washout surgery. He should have never had that surgery and then dealt with the wound vac.

What is the biggest blessing? Steve's answer is being alive, of course. It's hard for him to think of the positives as they directly relate to the amputation because he thinks about the physical limitations and the constant reminder.

My answer, hands down, is the relationship with Stacey, Steve's sister. I'm of the mindset that the only reason we have a relationship with her is because of the amputation. The other thing is that it changed the trajectory of my career, spurring me to share my passion of leaning into using natural solutions and living a holistic health lifestyle with the world.

Epilogue

If you only take one thing away from this book, let it be that you listen to your body and intuition. Always advocate for yourself – be it personally, professionally, or with your health. If you don't like an answer, get another opinion, and another, and another. Your brain is a powerful tool and your body is amazing. Don't take a diagnosis as your truth and certainly don't let it define who you are.

As I reflected back on the journey that Steve and I faced, it makes me appreciate where we are now. No, Steve shouldn't have had an amputation. We could point fingers and dwell in the what ifs, but that would only lead to an unhealthy spiral of depression and self-pity. We hold our heads high, knowing what Steve/our family overcame together, and are proud to have come through that awful, life-changing ordeal as better. Better because we remain positive. Better because Steve has adapted. Better because we're alive and genuinely choose happiness.

It's easy to quickly forget just how fragile life is. We get wrapped back up in the day-to-day trying to make ends meet and push the limits on our health, finances, and relationships. This is your gentle reminder, my friend. Be patient and kind with yourself and others. Live life to the fullest, trying to feel the deepest gratitude for everything you have.

I left my corporate job in January 2020 to pursue a career as an entrepreneur, as a holistic health and lifestyle advocate. My initial thoughts were to serve the amputee community, as

Steve and I developed protocols using natural solutions to help with skin care, phantom pain, wound care, and mental health. As the global pandemic took hold, I began to shift my thinking about what I thought people needed and what gifts God has blessed me with. My conclusion: my voice and desire to help people.

When I look back on what we went through and I see the uproar of our world, my ah-ha moment is when I realized the importance of self-care. I've transformed my company, Wellness Spoiled™, from timidly selling essential oils and related products to a self-care brand. My goal is to help demystify what self-care is and help you curate a personalized self-care routine that fills your cup day after day.

For my natural solution lovers, I still sell and educate people on how to take the overwhelm out of using essential oils, supplements, and toxin-free products, so that you can easily incorporate them into your lifestyle and self-care routines.

I have developed The Self-Care Method™ which is an easy way to start making self-care a part of your daily routine using The Self-Care Method™ Journal. You can also easily incorporate self-care by utilizing the tools in my self-care mobile app, Wellness Spoiled™, launching early 2023.

It would be an honor to help you on your wellness journey, so don't be a stranger!

www.WellnessSpoiled.com

@wellness.spoiled

@WellnessSpoiled 🇫

Tributes to Steve

photo credit: Nikki Brooker Photography

Thank you to our friends and family who have taken the time and put their hearts into the following messages to Steve. These heartfelt letters/notes/poems are their personal words and mean the world to our family. Thank you for your love and support through the years!

I don't remember a lot about my dad's amputation. I was in 4th grade and remember my parents not being around much. Over the years after it though, I have come to realize how amazing my dad is. He is way stronger than anyone I can imagine who goes through something like that. His mindset always seemed positive to me and I think it was. He didn't let the amputation limit his life. He still golfs and works.

Just recently he told me how out of shape he is, but I don't agree. I think it's amazing that he's able to work so long and not be completely gassed. I know that it is difficult for him sometimes, but he never lets it get him down. I'm so amazed and glad that he is able to go along like nothing ever happened.

I'm proud to call you dad.

Love you,
Talon

Steve,

When Danette told us she was authoring a book on the experiences and trials of losing your leg, I was really excited for you guys. I felt like it was probably extremely important for her to put her emotions into words, and it will maybe give you a perspective of the entire event through someone else's eyes. I know that for me, I hate even thinking about that time in your life and prefer to focus on all the cool times we get to have now and fun things we get to do. I will say though, that somehow you losing your leg has made you an even better golfer and even though I lose every round to you when we play, I am just pumped to get to share those experiences with you!

I recall visiting Littleton hospital with you and Danette when you had been experiencing pain in your lower leg/foot. I remember the doctors telling you they had no clue of what it was and there was really nothing they could do at that time. I cannot express how shocked I was when I found out that what they were unsure of, would result in you losing your leg. I certainly do not want to rehash the negative of that time, instead I would rather share my thoughts and feelings in a positive way. I cannot stress to you enough how tough you were/are and how that toughness is a constant reminder in my memories, when I think of you in there. Obviously, we grew up together and so I knew firsthand how tough you already were. I was amazed that everyday when I would visit, you would always be in high spirits and wanted to joke or just have a regular conversation, even though you were in unbearable pain. I would always tease you about being handicapped because that's how our relationship is and you always laughed or made fun of me right back. You never complained or seemed depressed in front of me. You never complained of the pain, you just dealt with it (sometimes with a grimace on your face) but you took punches and kept moving forward. To say how proud of you I was/am for handling that pain and always being positive around me, is just incredible. I remember that even though I hate hospitals and being in them, it was always a highlight in my day visiting because I got to hang out with you, even if for only 30-40 minutes some days. My favorite memory with you during that period, was the night I slept in your room at the hospital, so that we could watch the Cubs in the World Series on my iPad. I recall sneaking in a few beers and some Jack Daniels to make the experience of the game that much better lol! It was so cool to just have a fun night with you and give you some normalcy, even though you were in that shitty place.

You know me better than most and so you know I have a weak stomach for bodily injuries, etc. With that said, I remember taking you to a few appointments after you had gotten out of the hospital, and it was usually for repacking the wound etc. At one visit I remember I had to leave the room because I could not handle seeing your leg like that. I felt terrible because you are the one dealing with this process and I cannot even stomach being in the room. You never gave me grief, you never seemed upset, you never seemed offended, you never even made reference to it. I'm so lucky to have a brother who is that cool, all the while dealing with your overwhelming trauma. For you to be that strong and cool was something that I will always remember about that time we shared on doctor visits.

One thing I have learned is that life certainly is not fair, and you have to fight your ass off. It was not fair that your leg was taken, but you are still the same badass brother that you have always been, and your family is so incredibly lucky to have you in our lives. I love you bro and will look forward to the fun times ahead!

Scott

God had a plan for my brothers and me! He had to do it his way and in his time. So I stalked and watched from afar until the day came when I found out Steve had lost his leg! Something in my heart told me now was my time. I hate that it had to be this way but this was God's plan. I am so grateful to have you in my life now-love our talks...the serious ones and the ones that make me laugh! Your BIG smile, no matter how things are going and how you don't let anything stand in your way!

I Believe and Admire
How You Protect and Show
I Watch and Listen
You Love and Know
A Brothers Love
Is a Sisters Greatest Treasure
A Sisters Happiness
Is a Brothers Deepest Desire
Know that YOU ARE LOVED!

Love your Sister...Stacey xo

Dear Steve,

I will never forget the day of Peyton's 4ᵗʰ birthday party at Saddle Rock School of Gymnastics. I looked over and saw Danette and Talon arrive, but I didn't see you. I went to greet them and asked Danette where you were. When she said that something was wrong with your lower leg and foot, and you were literally laying on the floor in pain at home, I was shocked. I couldn't imagine what was wrong, and I felt so awful for you. None of us had any idea of the horrific experience that you were about to endure from that day forward.

Over the next several weeks, Scott and Danette would give me updates each day on how you were doing and what the doctors thought was the issue. I continued to be baffled by the mystery of what was going on, and why no one could figure it out. I remember being so amazed by you and how strong you were during that time. You were in so much pain, and most days you played it off like you were fine, even though you were probably dying inside. I can't imagine the stress you felt, going from doctor to doctor and hospital to hospital, not getting any answers. When it was finally determined that you needed to have your leg amputated, I couldn't believe it. I remember when Scott told me, I burst into tears. I couldn't believe that was truly the answer and the only solution. I kept hoping that another doctor would come into the picture and say there was another way. I couldn't imagine how you felt, hearing that you would lose your leg.

I remember sitting at the hospital for one of your surgeries and it took around three hours (or possibly longer). It was so nerve wracking, just waiting for any information from the doctors. I remember bringing papers to grade, so that I could take my mind off it, but it didn't do much. Danette was so strong and held it together so well. I was in awe of her and wondered if I would be able to do the same, had this been Scott. I don't know that I could. I just kept praying over and over to please let them fix your leg, and please don't let anything bad happen to you during surgery. There were fears that came into my mind that I don't even want to say, and none of us wanted to think about those fears. We just tried to stay positive and be there for you.

After the surgery when they took your leg, I was so nervous to see you in the hospital. I wasn't sure what I would say, how you would look, and what kind of visit it would be. I had no idea what to expect and I just hoped I wouldn't cry the whole time. I was so impressed by you that day. You were strong, upbeat, and positive. You were already making jokes and entertaining all the nurses. A joke came to my mind while I was there, and I thought, "Dare I say this joke? Is it too soon?" But it's you, so I went for it. With all the seriousness I could muster, I said, "Well, look on the bright side . . . maybe shoe stores will give you 50% off?" I was relieved when you started cracking up. But that is you – you are always ready for a laugh, and that didn't change even after one of the worst days of your life.

I am so proud of you for your strength in all of this. You continue to live your life every day, working hard and doing everything you can to support your family. You never complain about your leg, and you are always upbeat and positive. I can't imagine going through all that you did. It is very inspiring, and I continue to be impressed by you every day. I am lucky to have a brother-in-law like you. I love you!

Love,

Kara

Steve, the irony that you served your country in the Navy as a gunner and crew chief on helicopters without incident, only to lose part of your leg due to blood clots is uncanny. While spending some time with you shortly after the amputation, an emptiness in your heart was apparent. And yet, over the years, I see you have adapted very well, learning to drive with special controls, walking miles per day in your job, playing golf better than you ever had before, almost as if the situation had never occurred. Your attitude toward losing your leg was the key to recovery. I believe that you approached your situation daily with an optimism that your life would never be the same but possibly even better than ever and I am so honored to have you in our family and proud of your example.

Proud to have you part of our family!
Dad Caraway

Steve,

I couldn't be any prouder that you are my son-in-law, you are a true blessing. When your life was turned upside-down, your inner strength was greater than anything I could imagine or ever witnessed and, as a matter of fact, it's a characteristic of a **Hero**! This battlefield of life can be overwhelming at times and your strength and love was and is evident to everyone around you and continues to this day.

I love you and I am proud to call you, my Son!

I have observed how gracefully and gently you present yourself to others so there is no awkwardness. You stop and answer questions, and joke, when a stranger asks you "What Happened". You make it about their feelings and not about you. Selfless!

Thank you for coming into Danette's life and joining our family.

Friends, we need to be more like Steve.

Blessing today and always,

Caren Caraway

Dear Steve,
1.
We started as neighbors
Just barely a "hey there"
Just the nod of the head
Or a word or two said

We were neighbors, not friends
Busy lives was our trend
There's no time to get close
Not with them nor with those

And then one sunny day
A small boy was at play
He's so sweet and polite
Someone's raising him right

Who's his parents I say?
That young couple, OK
And a friendship took place
From that little round face

These young parents we met
But we didn't know yet
That we'd like them so much
Both our lives they would touch

Danette Penrod and Steve
They live just cross the street
With the tow-headed boy
To this day he's a joy

Talon Jon is his name
And he quickly became
Like a grandson to us
Never making a fuss

So, with these two young kids
Formed a friendship we did
Early on, we did find
That our values aligned

Sealed a friendship and bond
That today still holds strong
We've had dinners and beer
Gone to games where we'd cheer

2.
We've had fun and had laughs
Sharing food, games and drafts
And the fun didn't end
We met family and friends

We're as old as their folks
But they both have old souls
So, we quickly became
BFF's we would claim

Watched our Talon grow up
A wee lad, just a pup
Just as sweet as can be
A great kid we foresee

Now fast forward 6 years
Our good friend, he's in tears
There's a pain in his leg
They do scans and x-rays

But they find nothing wrong
Same old dance, same old song
Different docs and clinics
Diagnosis mimicked

After messing around
With these medical clowns
Who can't seem to find out
What this pain is about

And the pain's getting worse
Steve's beginning to curse
At the end of his rope
He can no longer cope

Then we finally found out
CU Doc's have no doubt
It's a blood clot they find
It was missed all those times

We can fix it they say
No, we won't amputate
Off to surgery you go
First of many although

3.
Not so easy they find
They continue the grind
With each surgery you hurt
The pain only gets worse

You hang tough as you can
You're a mighty strong man
But it came to a point
GET ME OUT OF THIS JOINT!

With your wife at your side
And your son close behind
You have ALL your support
You don't need any more

"Just do what you can
I will still be a man
With a whole leg or not
A brave fight I have fought"

"Get it DONE", you would say
Let's get going, TODAY
Take the leg, get it off
You had just had enough!

Let's just get it done
No more pain, "I want NONE"
Let's get rid of this pain
Get my life back again

You were strong, you were brave
That's the way you were raised
Round your friends and your wife
Until one early night

You had not seen your son
Had been quite a long run
When that sweet boy walked in
Tough veneer became thin

The tough strong man was gone
As he came to your arms
This pure love for your boy
All your hopes and your joy

4.
You just couldn't hold in
All the love you could give
Raw emotion we saw
A pure love that was raw

That's what makes you so strong
With the will to go on
Love of son, love of wife
Yes, you fight for your life!

A long road it has been
Just so much to take in
Six more years now have passed
You've continued, steadfast

You play golf and have fun
With your wife and your son
You are now the cool guy
Without having to try

"I can DO IT!" you say
Hanging tough every day
"So, I'm missing some leg"
"What the heck, what the hey"

You're still here and you're good
Got your life and manhood
Got your son and your wife
And a beautiful life

We don't think you deserve
That God threw you this curve
But you sure passed the test
You're still here, we're all blessed

An example you've set
Yes, the challenge you've met
You stood up, you stood strong
And you've continued on

We're so glad you're our friend
Lots of good times ahead
Hope this message is clear
We feel blessed that you're here!

With all our LOVE,
Jerry and Laurie

Steve is an inspiration in the way he has dealt with his amputation. He has fought through adversity with his own sense of humor and sarcasm. He has been blessed to have the love and support from his wife, son, family, and by so many friends. So many memories of the past 6 years...

- I remember the Air Force v. Navy game before the amputation where he was not going to let the pain stop him from being with his friends. I don't recall who won that game but will not forget his toughness or what others may call his stubbornness.
- I remember him struggling to have a beer shortly before the surgery when we visited him after a round of golf, but Steve would not let his friends drink alone. I think it may have been the one and only time he did not finish his beer.
- I remember the pirate cake, parrot, and eye patch the night before and admired his tenacity and determination. *Pirate Steve* was born that night.
- I'll never forget our road trip back to Wisconsin where we created memories and stories we'll tell for years to come; first round of golf with the new prosthetic, cold showers, wood ticks, playing pool, and laughing for hours.
- I also remember when I used to be able to beat Stave at golf, but those days are long gone now! Good news is that I can still beat him in a race as he was never very fast even with 2 legs!

I am grateful to call Steve my friend and am thankful to have him in my life. Love ya!
- Jeff

When the reality of losing his leg set in, Steve was able to use his sense of humor and sarcasm to help make that conversation more productive with his family (thank God for an incredible wife) and doctors. Although it was life altering, he managed to own it and move forward to ensure he stuck around a lot longer for all that loved him. I still think of the pirate cake, eye patch, and parrot the night before the procedure, and was amazed with how well he was taking it all in. Can't imagine a life without Steve to keep us all laughing, amused, and on our toes. - Love you Bud – Holly